The Educational Manager

Artist and Practitioner

The Educational Manager

Artist and Practitioner

E. G. Bogue
Tennessee Higher Education Commission
Robert L. Saunders
Memphis State University

Charles A. Jones Publishing Company
Worthington, Ohio

To

Truman M. Pierce
Dean, School of Education
Auburn University

and

John W. Richardson, Jr.
Former Dean, Graduate School
Memphis State University

Who exemplify the artistic approach
to educational management

1   2   3   4   5   6   7   8   9   10   /   79   78   77   76

Library of Congress Catalog Card Number: 75-12016
International Standard Book Number: 0-8396-0057-7

Printed in the United States of America

Preface

Improving the effectiveness of educational management is the unifying theme of *The Educational Manager*. It is based on three convictions. The first is that performance of our educational institutions is directly related to the quality of their management. The second is that a sure command and application of management concepts will lead to more effective performance. And the third is that educational managers must have as much concern for the goals of their institutions as they do for the ways by which those goals are achieved. The book provides tools and techniques by which the administrator can improve performance and reach his goals effectively.

It provides interpretation of theory, but also tells how to implement that theory. It shows the manager as a creative practitioner who skillfully applies management principles, using authority effectively yet sensitively. It tells how he can balance control with independence by using a flexible managerial style. To help each manager develop his own unique skills, the book . . .

   . . . shows how the manager can be an artist, an organizer of talents.

   . . . points out the complexity of his role and responsibilities.

   . . . demonstrates how ideas can be the means for effective administration.

A manager must do more than keep pace with his work; he must plan, execute, evaluate. This book provides a guide for his continuing drive for improving education. Each chapter deals with both the goals of education and ways of achieving those goals. Questions at the ends of the chapters relate concepts to actual managerial tasks.

Problems are the manager's opportunities; they enable him to right wrongs, to heal wounds—to practice the art of management. The book explains how to meet challenges. It also tells how the manager can allocate his own time creatively, permitting long-range planning that will reduce future problems.

The Educational Manager shows how good theory, applied practically and sensitively, can help the manager every day. It shows how to unify the *purpose* and *process* of education. The result, better educational management, is vital.

Contents

1

Improving Management Effectiveness

*Management is, all things considered, the most
creative of all arts. It is the art of arts, because it is
the organizer of talent.*

Jean-Jacques Servan-Schreiber

What are the elements of role and responsibility that mark the
work of the educational manager? Certainly a different mix of
technical, human relations, and conceptual skills distinguishes
the work of the college department chairman from that of the
university president and the role of the school principal from that
of the superintendent. Yet there are some common elements of
role and responsibility that are an integral part of the work of any
educational manager.

The behavior and conversation of the newly appointed educational manager may not betray the inward question which all
ask: "What am I supposed to do?" We have known a number of
educational managers, some of them freshly minted from degree
programs and others who were 20-year veterans with one year's
experience, who did not know where to start, who had little
understanding of their role and its relation to those with whom
they worked. An examination of role and responsibility is the first
step in our reflection on managerial concepts.

Role and Responsibility - A Historical Perspective

Claude S. George indicates that the roots of management
thought can be traced back to 4000-5000 B. C.[1] The political and
engineering triumphs of ancient civilizations tell us that the
achievements of those civilizations would hardly have been
possible without some application of organizational and
administrative concepts. A host of writings have touched on the
work of managers prior to the 20th century. For example, in one

of the classics that still is required reading in most management programs, we find Niccolo Machiavelli suggesting that one who governs must be:

> . . . both feared and loved, but as it is difficult for the two to go together, it is much safer to be feared than loved, if one of the two has to be wanting.[2]

And this piece of advice is complemented as follows:

> How laudable it is for a prince to keep good faith and live with integrity, and not with astuteness, everyone knows. Still the experience of our times shows those princes have done great things who have had little regard for good faith, and have been able by astuteness to confuse men's brains, and who have ultimately overcome those who have made loyalty their foundation.[3]

The systematic study of management thought is generally agreed to have begun in the 20th century. The first complete theory of management thought was articulated early in the 20th century by a French engineer, Henri Fayol, who observed that management was an activity common to all human undertakings. He proposed that management activity of all kinds could be factored into five components:

Planning —	Building a plan of action and setting goals.
Organizing —	Structuring human and material resources to put the plan into action.
Commanding —	Maintaining the plan in action.
Coordinating —	Unifying and harmonizing work efforts.
Controlling —	Ensuring that activity moves in accordance with the plan.[4]

Variations on this theme may be found. For example, to the functions outlined by Fayol, Luther Gulick added the activities of staffing, reporting, and budgeting.[5] Russell Gregg perceives seven steps in the process.[6]

1. Decision Making
2. Planning

3. Organizing
4. Communicating
5. Influencing
6. Coordinating
7. Evaluating

In another of the classics in the history of management thought, Chester Barnard proposed that the fundamental managerial function is that of "maintaining systems of cooperative effort."[7] The supporting activities related to this function are in his words "first, to provide the system of communication; second, to promote the securing of essential efforts; and third, to formulate and define purpose."[8]

Paul F. Lazarsfeld takes the position that managers (he uses the term administrators) in all organizations are confronted by four major tasks. He outlines them as follows:

1. The administrator must fulfill the *goals* of the organization.
2. The administrator must make use of *other people* in fulfilling these goals, not as if they were machines, but rather in such a way as to release their initiative and creativity.
3. The administrator must also face the humanitarian aspects of his job. He wants people who work for him to be happy. This is *morale*—the idea that under suitable conditions people will do better work than they will under unsuitable conditions.
4. The administrator must try to build into his organization provisions for innovations, for change, and for development. In a changing world, people and organizations must adjust to changing conditions. The conditions for change must be incorporated into the organization so that there may be a steady process of development rather than a series of sudden, disruptive innovations.[9]

In one of the really fine resources to appear in recent years, Jacob W. Getzels and others contend that the manager is "to integrate the expectations of the institution and the dispositions of the individuals in such a way that it is at once organizationally fruitful and individually satisfying."[10]

Finally, in a contemporary and widely read book, Robert R. Blake and Jane S. Mouton tell us that:

> . . . a manager's job is to perfect a culture which (1) promotes and sustains efficient performance of highest quality and quantity; (2) fosters and utilizes creativity; (3) stimulates enthusiasm for effort, experimentation, innovation, and change; (4) takes educational advantage from interaction situations and; (5) looks for and finds new challenges.[11]

Can we distill this scholarship into a guide for action? What points of agreement can we find on the role of the manager? Can we cast them in a concise format for the educational manager seeking to know more clearly the domain of his responsibility?

A simple and forceful synthesis is given by Peter Drucker who suggests that the manager is expected "to get the right things done."[12] It is doubtful that we will improve upon the power of this definition, for it includes the element of action and efficiency (get things *done*) and also the element of effectiveness (get the *right* things done). However, we feel that the four elements we propose below give a concise description of the role of the educational manager.

Role and Responsibility - A Current Perspective

Goal Setting and Goal Adaptation

The first and primary function of any manager, educational or business, is to ensure that the goals of his organization are clearly stated and understood. James G. Harlow has suggested that "purpose-defining" is the central function of the school administrator.[13] How are the goals of the elementary school in the small rural town the same as those of a similar type of school in the ghetto? And how are the goals for a department of chemistry in a small liberal arts college distinguished from the goals of a similar department in a large urban university? Are they the same?

Definition and communication of goals must be followed by continued attention to goal review and revision. The goals of a high school may not be the same in 1970 as they were in 1960. Similarly, the goals of a university may not be the same when it has an enrollment of 20,000 as when it had an enrollment of 5,000. Educational management ensures that goals respond to the changing environment.

Resource Acquisition and Allocation

The second major responsibility of educational management is the acquisition of resources—both human and material—and the effective allocation of them to the defined purposes. Of course the degree to which different managers are involved in resource acquisition varies. The school principal may expend less of his energy in this activity than his superintendent, and the department chairman or dean may expend less time and energy than the college president. But no matter what the position, each manager finds himself confronted with the responsibility of determining resource needs, of justifying these needs, and of ensuring that resources are equitably and effectively applied.

Resource Organization

Designing an effective and efficient arrangement of human and material resources constitutes still another critical responsibility of educational management. This responsibility includes an obligation to integrate individuals with organization and *to match talent with task* so that the most effective mix of individual needs and organizational purpose is achieved. Though the motive force in our schools and colleges emerges from the force of individual personality, the way in which we organize our human resources is an important determinant of individual productivity and satisfaction.

Organization of technological resources is also a part of this responsiblity. The education profession has been severely criticized because productivity in this field has not shown the same increase as in business and industry. Educators are still debating whether it is appropriate or even possible to apply the productivity concept to the educational process. But we do not have to await the resolution of that argument to realize that the timely application of technology can enhance both the efficiency and effectiveness of our schools and colleges. Effective organization is a mark of managerial intelligence and artistry.

Program and Personnel Evaluation

Purposes are defined and plans of action drawn. Resources are acquired and allocated. An organizational structure is devised. What remains for the educational manager? The truth is that some managers are quite willing to cease functioning at this point. They assume that all will now go according to plan. But reality violates this assumption. Every good plan requires follow-up evaluation to ensure that all is moving according to plan or to learn that the plan was ill-advised or incomplete.

Too often—perhaps most often—evaluation is viewed as something that happens once a year, deals only with individuals, and serves primarily to define a base for salary increments.

However, as one writer in educational evaluation has suggested, evaluation is a continuous process of assessing how well actions match intent, and of indentifying discrepancies between what was planned and what actually happened.[14] No meaningful evaluation of outcomes is possible unless we can be sure that educational plans were executed as intended or unless we can detect unforeseen consequences of plans through continuous evaluation and correct them. Thus the effective manager knows that evaluation is an ongoing activity affecting not only personnel but programs as well.

Evaluative responsiblity means that the educational manager must design and implement an effective follow-up and feedback system. But such a system requires two other elements—a clear set of goals and a clear set of criteria by which performance is to be measured. And, this brings us full circle to the original responsibility of goal setting and adaptation.

The four responsibilities we have outlined are not necessarily sequential. That is, one does not first say that one will define goals, then acquire resources, then organize, and finally, evaluate, The process is an interacting and ongoing one.

Let us recall the concise definition of role borrowed from Drucker—that management responsibility is to get the right things done. What barriers are there to more effective performance and what contribution can this book make to overcoming these barriers?

Barriers to Effectiveness

Inadequate Role Concept

One of the principal barriers to more effective performance is that educational managers often do not have a clear concept of what they are supposed to do. For example, some managers—principals and presidents, directors and deans—become absorbed in the doing of management. They begin to think of themselves as some magnificent combination of coach, quarterback, guard, and halfback. They design the plays and also call the signals. They clear the way, tackle problems headon and make stellar broken field runs through faculty and students. This concept of role ignores, however, the important fact that one cannot manage and operate simultaneously.

Another version of the ineffective manager is the one who expends his energy in managerial "clucking." There is probably a more scholarly description for this behavior, but we are thinking of the manager who is commanded by his inbasket, rushes about in a frenzy checking locks on doors and the number of forms in stock, and never gets far enough away from "administrivia" to see if his organization is moving toward a healthy set of goals.

Thus, some managers clearly see the operational details before them, but have little or no conception of where the operation is moving. Some claim they cannot find the time for planning and goal setting. They have failed to realize that one of the most important resources the manager must allocate is his own time. He may make plans during an hour early in the morning, a few moments at the office in which he schedules no appointments, or an evening at the office.

Whatever the time of day or style he employs, every manager needs time for planning, for "direction reflection." Finding it will not be easy. For the greater his management responsibilities are, the more his time will be commanded by the appointment calendar. However, a careful screening of that calendar often reveals some demands that are not highly essential and others that can be more quickly and effectively dispatched by another member of the management staff.

This problem of managing time has been forcefully put by Eugene Jennings as he speaks of the need for leadership in contemporary organizations. Speaking of the leader as the "superior man," Jennings suggests that the superior man's

> . . . greatest struggle is against the annihilation of his privacy. Where the typical executive has somehow managed to persuade himself that he is too busy to think, to read, to look back and forward, the superior man places a high value upon thought. Private deliberation is next to impossible for the executive because his working day is so cluttered with group meetings, conferences, formal and informal committees, that he has no privacy left. He has become a living automaton at the mercy of anyone who can pick up a telephone or put his face in the door or push the panic button sounding the alarm for another committee meeting.[15]

Inadequate Knowledge Base

The term "professional" implies a foundation of knowledge. Yet some educational managers still insist that there is nothing serious to be known about managing a school or college. One college president, just prior to his nonvoluntary resignation, frequently observed that concepts of administration had little to do with running a university. He operated under the assumption that his experience as a professor and department head were sufficient preparation for his work as president. We are not arguing that these experiences do not provide a set of sensitivities important to the college presidency, but rather that they usually are not sufficient in themselves. One is not automatically invested with the knowledge and skill required to be an effective educational manager by virtue of having been a teacher or faculty member or even having held another administrative post.

This is not a good time for "seat-of-the-pants" management in schools and colleges. There is a body of concepts and ideas to be commanded by those who aspire to direct our schools and colleges, and those ignorant of its existence are not likely to perform effectively.

Inadequate Artistry in Managerial Action

There are some educational managers who know their roles and who have the knowledge necessary to carry them out, but who fail the last test—the test of performance. We cannot say that the only barriers to effective performance are those of inadequate role concept and inadequate knowledge base. The impediments to effective performance are not quite that simple.

Some managers find *themselves* a barrier to more effective performance. They are very much like the comic strip character Pogo who observed on one occasion, "We have met the enemy and he is us." These managers lack a clear concept of personal identity. They are affected too much by whatever pressure is on them at the moment, swayed by the whim of person and event. They shrink from hard decisions and substitute policy for courage. Still other managers find themselves in roles which are totally at variance with their talents and interests.

Ideas in Action - A Key to Effectiveness

We have looked at the obligations of the educational manager and also identified some of those barriers which impede his effectiveness in meeting those obligations. In this summary discussion, and throughout the remainder of the book, our intent is to emphasize the power of ideas in the improvement of performance.

The educational manager needs at his command two kinds of ideas. He needs first a solid foundation of scientific concepts, for as Harry Levinson reminds us:

> A professional is a person who must understand and apply scientific knowledge. Unless he does so, he will be buffeted by forces beyond his control. Given knowledge, the professional can choose courses of action; he remains in charge of himself and his work.[16]

The mark of the professional, then, is that his actions are guided by knowledge. But he needs more than scientific concepts. The experienced educational manager knows that he also needs a carefully constructed and clearly understood value framework. Failure to fashion a personal value system causes the manager operational headaches.

> Without philosophic orientation, educational leaders take one of several directions, the administrator relinquishes his leadership role, expends his energies in dealing with the routines of management, and deludes himself that this is really his chief function. He swims madly, albeit without direction through a sea of school-management minutiae.[17]

Thus, the educational manager needs both scientific and normative ideas. Unfortunately, the managerial theorist and the managerial practictioner frequently toss verbal "darts" at one another. The scholar/theoretician stands on the mountain top of ideas and looks down at the practictioner with a kind of condescending detachment. And down in the valley of practice, the manager on the firing line has little patience with the theorist who has his head "stuck in the clouds."

That the work of one is essential and complementary to that of the other often escapes their attention. The city school superintendent caught up in a social or economic controversy and the college president with a student revolt on his hands certainly are operating at the heart of professional service. But the scholar on the remote outpost of ideas also serves, for the practictioner may be marching to the power of his ideas for the next hundred years.

Intelligence and creativity are required for both roles. Few school principals or university deans would aspire to make the conceptual contribution of an Einstein or of any other major theorist. However, it is at least questionable whether Einstein would have made a very effective college dean. It is reported that when the famous French mathematician Laplace took over the reins of French governmental finance, the government almost went broke. Apparently, the kind of intelligence and creativity required for theoretical work in mathematics was not necessarily the same as the intelligence and creativity required for managing governmental finance.

What we propose is a cooperative bond between the world of ideas and the world of action. We contend that the effective professional has his actions anchored in knowledge—knowledge of himself, knowledge of his role, and knowledge of the environment in which he performs.

To illustrate the point, let us examine briefly just one set of ideas and see how these ideas contribute to improved performance. In the recent history of management thought, there have been few propositions more common in the literature than the one flowing originally from the research work of C.L. Shartle in the Ohio State University leadership studies. In an examination of the role and behavior of many kinds of managers, two fundamental factors emerged—a concern for task and a concern for person. These two factors were named "initiation of structure" and "consideration." Figure 1 shows how variations of this basic idea are laced throughout the work of more recent writers.

What does the scholarship cited in Figure 1 tell us? Certainly more than can be captured in a paragraph. But consider these as examples of some of the implications for the practicing manager. First, it is clear, principally from the Getzels and Guba model, that conflict can emerge when the expectations of followers differ from those of the leader. A person-centered style would not be highly effective in an environment in which followers were expecting high authority.

Second, there is a relationship between management style and task environment. A task-centered style may be completely ineffective in an environment where the success of group production depends upon close and cooperative interactions. There is a relationship between personality and dominant management style. Many managers will have a tendency toward either task-centered or person-centered style.

Thus, the effective manager needs, according to Reddin, three skills: situational sensitivity skill, style flexibility skill, and situational management skill. In essence, then, the effective manager learns to judge the management environment in

Figure 1. The Presence of Task- and Person-Centered Variables
in Management Scholarship

Author and Reference	Task Variable	Person Variable
C.L. Shartle *Executive Performance and Leadership* (1956)[18]	Initiating Structure	Consideration
J.W. Getzels and E.G. Guba "Social Behavior & the Administrative Process" (1957)[19]	Nomothetic Dimension	Idiographic Dimension
Robert R. Blake and Jane Srygley Mouton *The Managerial Grid* (1964)[20]	Concern for Production	Concern for Persons
F.E. Fiedler *A Theory of Leadership Effectiveness* (1967)[21]	Task Structure	Leader Member Relations
W.J. Reddin *Managerial Effectiveness* (1970)[22]	Task Orientation	Relations Orientation

which he finds himself, to adapt his style to the people and the place, and to adjust the environment where possible. All of these concepts will appear again throughout this book.

Management and Administration— A Postscript on Meaning

Before leaving this chapter, we should attend briefly to one other matter. Most books that treat the topic of management/administration in the field of education use the term "administration." Why then have we chosen the term "management" for our title, but suggest in the Preface that the terms administration and management have an equivalent meaning.

First, many writers—in educational administration, in public administration, and in business administration—have used and do use the terms interchangeably. For example, in the index of one of the better known texts in business management we will find the phrase "see management" under the term "administration."[23] The same practice is found in the field of public administration. An early text in the field is entitled *Management in the Public Service,*[24] and we can fnd the same terminology in later references.[25] Yet when one gets into the substance of these books, and others like them, it is obvious that the terms administration and management are used synonymously.

For the most part, then, the two words are given the same meaning. There are a few writers who choose to make some distinction. For example, in *Management: Tasks, Responsibilities, Practices,* Peter Drucker makes such a distinction, suggesting that administration is a part of management.[26] He indicates that the administrative job of the manager is to optimize the use of resources but does not see administration as having any responsibility for innovation. Parenthetically, we note that Drucker reinforces our theme that management is not just a science, but is practice based on both science and values.[27] In a book previously cited in this chapter, Reddin also makes a distinction by saying that "Administration suggests maintaining a going concern with little actual change in key elements such as organization philosophy or technology."[28]

Other writers also encourage the notion that management is a more inclusive term than administration by subsuming leadership as a component of management. For example, in their text on organizational theory, James L. Gibson and others indicate that leadership "is one of the mechanisms called upon to serve the management function . . . ."[29] And in his widely known book on human relations, Keith Davis suggests that "leadership is a part of management, but not all of it."[30] Thus, both of these, and others see leadership as a dimension of management.

The reason for administration being conceived as a part of management can be traced back to the turn of the century. Scholars from Woodrow Wilson on tended to create a distinction between policy-making and administration—a dichotomy still held by some contemporary writers and practitioners. We believe this to be a false distinction and one not found in the practice of those who hold responsibility in any field of public administration or management. We agree with Harlan Cleveland, writing in his book *The Future Executive,* that "now the public executives don't just implement; they initiate."[31] This concept will be discussed again in Chapter 9.

To emphasize our conviction that the educational manager has leadership responsibility for goal setting and policy-making, we have chosen to use the term "management" rather than "administration" in most of this discussion. However, we do not wish to generate unnecessary and unproductive arguments over the meaning of the two terms, since they are so frequently used with synonymous meaning. Those readers who prefer the term "administration" will find that we use it frequently in this book. And where the term "management" is found, the term "administration" may be freely substituted without damage to the meaning we hope to convey.

The posture taken in this book is the same as that taken several years ago by Ordway Tead who suggested that application of management concepts to specific situations "surely comprises an art requiring great skill, discernment, and moral fortitude."[32] It is the same also as the conviction of David E. Lilienthal, a founder of TVA and former chairman of the Atomic Energy Commission, who said:

> The art of management in these terms is a high form of leadership, for it seeks to combine the act—the getting of something done—with the meaining behind the act. The manager-leader would combine in one personality the robust, realistic quality of the man of action with the insight of the artist, the religious leader, the poet, who explain man to himself, who inspire man to great deeds and incredible stamina. The man of action alone, nor the man of contemplation alone, will not be enough in the situations we now confront; these two qualities together are required to meet the world's need for leadership.[33]

Summary

Some contemporary writers allude to management as a science. And, indeed, management must rest on a scientific foundation. But at this stage of management scholarship, there is no one theory sufficient in breadth to provide a single framework of action. In creating the most effective organization of task, talent, and technology, the educational manager is artist as well, a professional with a solid command of social-behavioral concepts which he places in action with a special sensitivitiy to both people and place.

The remaining chapters of this book will treat those ideas, concepts, knowledges that seem essential prerequisites to more effective performance. And since the book is written for the "firing-line" educational manager, he will have opportunities for testing in action the validity of concepts found here.

DISCUSSION QUESTIONS/LEARNING ACTIVITIES

1. Robert Hutchins once said, "The administrator must accept a special responsibility for the discovery, clarification, definition and proclamation of the end (the purpose of the institution). But he does not own the institution." What is your interpretation of this statement?

2. Select one educational management position well known to you—college president, school superintendent, school principal or college dean—and think of the different groups that have certain expectations for the person who occupies this position. In what way would you expect the role expectations to be different among the groups you identify?

3. Do you know of an educational manager who moved from a position where he was considered to be very effective to another in which he was considered to be very ineffective? To what factors do you attribute his lack of success?

4. Identify one educational manager who you feel manages his time in an effective way. How does this manager find time for planning and reflection?

5. Interview several practicing educational managers. In these interviews see if you can determine (a) how many of these can clearly articulate the goals and objectives of his institution or activity and (b) how many can identify those indicators they use to assess their own effectiveness as educational managers.

6. Interview professors teaching in the fields of educational administration, business administration, and public administration. What are their perceptions of the meaning of the two terms "management" and "administration?" Do these perceptions differ in any significant way?

NOTES

1. Claude S. George, Jr., *The History of Management Thought* (Englewood Cliffs, N.J.: Prentice-Hall, 1968).

2. Niccolo Machiavelli, *The Prince and the Discourses* (New York: The Modern Library, 1950), p. 61.

3. *Ibid.,* p. 63.

4. Henri Fayol, *General and Industrial Management* (London: Sir Isaac Pitman & Sons, 1949), pp. 6-7.

5. Luther Halsey Gulick and L. Urwick, *Papers on the Science of Administration* (New York: Institute of Public Administration, 1937), p. 13.

6. Russell T. Gregg, "The Administrative Process" in *Administrative Behavior in Education,* eds., Roald Campbell and Russell T. Gregg (New York: Harper & Row, 1957), pp. 269-317.

7. Chester I. Barnard, *The Functions of the Executive* (Cambridge: Harvard University Press, 1966), p. 216.

8. *Ibid.,* p. 217.

9. Paul F. Lazarsfeld, "The Social Sciences and Administration: A Rationale," in *The Social Sciences and Educational Administration,* eds., Lorne Downey and Frederick Enns (Edmonton: University of Alberta, 1963), pp. 3-4.

10. Jacob W. Getzels and others, *Educational Administration As A Social Process* (New York: Harper & Row, 1968), p. 119.

11. Robert R. Blake and Jane Srygley Mouton, *The Managerial Grid* (Houston: Gulf Publishing, 1964) p. x.

12. Peter Drucker, *The Effective Executive* (New York: Harper & Row, 1967), p. 1.

13. James G. Harlow, "Purpose Defining: The Central Function of the School Administrator," in *Preparing Administrators: New Perspectives,* eds., Jack A. Culbertson and Stephen P. Hencley (Columbus, O.: University Council for Educational Administration, 1962), pp. 61-77.

14. Malcolm Provus, *Discrepancy Evaluation* (Berkeley, Calif.: McCutchan, 1971).

15. Eugene E. Jennings, *An Anatomy of Leadership: Princes, Heroes and Supermen* (New York: McGraw-Hill, 1960), p. 141.

16. Harry Levinson, *The Exceptional Executive: A Psychological Conception* (Cambridge: Harvard University Press, 1968), p. 1.

17. Orin B. Graff, Calvin M. Street, Ralph B. Kimbrough and Archie R. Dykes, *Philosophic Theory and Practice in Educational Administration* (Belmont, Calif.: Wadsworth, 1966), p. 10.

18. Carroll Leonard Shartle, *Executive Performance and Leadership* (Englewood Cliffs, N.J.: Prentice-Hall, 1956).

19. Jacob W. Getzels and E. G. Guba, "Social Behavior and the Administrative Process," *School Review,* 65 (1957), pp. 423-441.

20. Blake and Mouton, *The Managerial Grid,* p. 8.

21. Fred E. Fiedler, *A Theory of Leadership Effectiveness* (New York: McGraw-Hill, 1967), pp. 133-153.

22. William J. Reddin, *Managerial Effectiveness* (New York: McGraw-Hill, 1970), p. 13.

23. Justin G. Longenecker, *Principles of Management and Organizational Behavior* (Columbus, O.: Charles E. Merrill, 1973), p. 697.

24. John D. Millett, *Management in the Public Service* (New York: McGraw-Hill, 1954).

25. For an example, see Robert T. Golembieski, ed., *Perspectives on Public Management: Cases and Learning Designs* (Itasca, Ill.: F. E. Peacock, 1968).

26. Peter F. Drucker, *Management: Tasks, Responsibilities, Practices* (New York: Harper & Row, 1974), pp. 45-47.

27. *Ibid.,* p. 17.

28. Reddin, *Managerial Effectiveness,* p. 160.

29. James L. Gibson, John M. Ivancevich, James H. Donnelly, Jr., *Organizations: Structure, Processes, Behavior* (Dallas: Business Publications, 1973), p. 285.

30. Keith Davis, *Human Behavior at Work* (New York: McGraw-Hill, 1972), p. 101.

31. Harlan Cleveland, *The Future Executive* (New York: Harper & Row, 1972), p. xi.

32. Ordway Tead, *The Art of Administration* (New York: McGraw-Hill, 1951), p.4.

33. David E. Lilienthal, *Management: A Humanist Art* (New York: Carnegie Institute of Technology, Distributed by Columbia University Press, 1967), p. 17.

2

The Determinants of Organizational Behavior

*No book will ever make a wise man out of a donkey
or a genius out of an incompetent . . . No discipline
can lengthen a man's arm. But it can lengthen his
reach by hoisting him on the shoulders of his
predecessors. Knowledge organized in a discipline
does a good deal for the merely competent; it endows
him with some effectiveness. It does infinitely more
for the truly able; it endows him with excellence.*

Peter Drucker, *Managing for Results*

Since the German sociologist Max Weber first outlined the characteristics of a bureaucracy, the literature on organizational theory has been growing with exponential rapidity. The recent books by Bernard M. Bass,[1] Victor Thompson,[2] William G. Scott,[3] and J. G. March[4] show the interest in this relatively new field of inquiry. Moreover, a variety of disciplines are participating in both separate and interdisciplinary ventures into organizational inquiry. Economists, sociologists, psychologists, management specialists, educators, and mathematicians have initiated studies in one or more phases of organizational theory.

For the educational manager, the array of research and reporting in organizational theory presents a dilemma not unlike that faced by the teacher confronting the literature of educational psychology. From the research and writing of the behavioral, stimulus-response, cognitive, neuro-physiological, and developmental psychologists, the teacher searches for those conceptual threads which he may weave into the fabric

This chapter has been adapted from the article "The Context of Organizational Behavior: A Conceptual Synthesis for the Educational Administrator" in the Spring 1969 issue of *Educational Administration Quarterly,* pp. 58-75. Used by permission.

of his classroom teaching. Constructing a conceptual framework which can serve as a guide to more enlightened practice proves to be a formidable task.

A similar challenge faces the educational manager as he surveys the literature of organizational theory, which is as diverse as that of educational psychology. The orchestration of personnel, material resources, and ideas which leads to the harmonious integration of man and organization is a complex task. It is natural, therefore, that the practicing educational manager would also search for those concepts and principles which would assist him in developing a more commanding professional competency.

There are considerable risks in any attempt to distill the numerous points of inquiry found in organizational theory. Entire books have dealt with the topics of job satisfaction, motivation, communication, supervisory behavior, organizational conflict, and decision-making processes. A chapter of this length can hardly capture the full impact of these topics, but it can consider a portion of organizational inquiry of immediate utility to the practitioner—whether he be an elementary school principal, school superintendent, or university president.

The principal focus of the chapter is the determinants of organizational behavior. We will suggest a simple model composed of four elements and then examine the relation of each element to individual behavior. The reader will readily discern considerable interaction among the elements, but for purposes of exposition we have chosen to treat them separately. Our objective is to provide a concise conceptual framework of value to the educational manager.

A Simplified Model
of Behavior Determinants

In the literature of organizational theory, one can find research and theory related to a number of organizational concepts. Since this chapter is an attempt to capsule some of these concepts into a more concise scheme, we present a highly simplified model involving four elements.

As Figure 2 indicates, we suggest that individual behavior in organizations can be viewed in terms of four perspectives:

Figure 2. Simplified Model of Behavior Determinants

Individual Behavior Within Organizations			
Management Philosophy	Organizational Structure	Group Membership	Individual Personality

management philosophy, organizational structure, group membership, and individual personality. Each of these elements has important implications for practice as the educational manager develops structures and relationships designed to free the creative energies of those with whom he works.

The Influence of Management Philosophy

The thesis in this discussion is that management philosophy is a key variable in influencing individual behavior within the organization. In treating management philosophy, we intend to consider those value dispositions and assumptions which managers hold about the nature of man and his work. We will suggest that management philosophy has changed significantly over the past half century, primarily as a result of intense research into the nature of leadership and organizations.

Three rather distinct periods of thought can be discerned in the literature of administration and management. The first is often called "scientific management." Scientific management was born in the late 19th century and flourished in the early 20th century, principally as a result of the research and writing of Frederick Taylor.[5] Based predominantly on the philosophy of Adam Smith, scientific management focused on the economic nature of man. In essence, scientific management embraced the study of work specialization and wage analysis. Jobs were dissected in order to find the most efficient way of doing a particular task and to set a fair wage. Some of the assumptions about the nature of the average worker were not very noble, and the central theme was that money was the principal motivator.

Although its influence began to wane in the 1920s, scientific management produced a number of more effective management practices. Industrial psychologists found that the problem of motivation-satisfaction was not as simple as the economic model which was assumed by scientific management. At the Western Electric Company, the now familiar Hawthorne studies by Elton Mayo and his colleagues destroyed many hallowed assumptions about the attitudes of workers toward their jobs. These and other studies also punched large holes in the concept of an organization as a blueprint in action—a series of line and staff relationships with fixed job responsibilities and closely specified interrelationships as initially proposed by Max Weber.

Organizations were revealed as social systems composed of both formal and informal elements, of grapevines and cliques, of overt and covert power structures, and of both logical and nonlogical behavioral patterns. The economic assumption of the scientific-management era was not adequate to account for the diverse need patterns uncovered, some of which were the psychological needs for recognition, for security, for accomplishment, and for involvement.

Out of the research of the industrial psychologists in the 1920s and 1930s emerged the "human relations" movement. This movement stressed the notion that if managers became more sensitive to the diversity of human needs, they could deal more effectively with the problems of motivation and conflict within organizations.

A host of training and development programs in human relations were developed for executives and supervisors. Reaching its zenith in the 1950s, the movement thereafter began to lose some of its momentum, but it was the first to introduce in a systematic way the findings of behavioral science into management practice, and this represents no small contribution. Perhaps its demise in recent years may be attributed to a lack of hard research validating the effectiveness of human relations training and to the inhospitable environment to which many managers returned after being trained in human relations.

"Industrial humanism" is the rubric which describes the current trend in management philosophy.[6] The writings of scholars such as Chris Argyris, Douglas McGregor, and Rensis Likert provide much of the empirical and theoretical bases for this movement. Relying heavily upon the hierarchical need structure proposed by the psychologist Abraham S. Maslow, these theorists have suggested a number of concepts which merit serious reflection.

Maslow proposed a hierarchy of human needs beginning with the basic physiological needs and culminating in the higher social and ego needs, such as need for self-actualization.[7] The need for self-actualization can be described as a desire to feel that one's abilities are being fully utilized in some worthwhile and creative manner. We shall see how this theory makes a contribution to contemporary management philosophy.

One of the traditional assumptions about man and his work has been that man is generally opposed to work. Notions of control and authority therefore occupied prominent positions in traditional management philosophy. Scholars of the industrial humanist movement suggest that restrictive managerial control, coupled with inadequate opportunities for self-actualization, inhibits the development of trust among managers and between managers and employees. This paucity of trust and honesty in human relationships leads to serious dysfunctional consequences.

An experienced administrator has observed such dysfunctional consequences many times. Consider the following example of how trust and communication may be related. If no feeling of trust exists between the administration and the employee, then communication is filtered as information moves both up and down in the organizational hierarchy. The results are as follows. Failure to communicate downward means that employees cannot relate their individual and group objectives to the overall organizational objectives. Failure of employees to communicate upward means that the administrator does not receive accurate information about the true status of organizational operations. Eventually, of course, organizational productivity is affected.

We can begin to see how the motivation psychology of Maslow has had an impact on management philosophy, for Maslow has suggested that once the physiological needs are satisfied, the higher level needs become operative. Opportunity for self-actualization—for using his full array of talents in a creative venture—may transform work into an activity from which the individual may derive real pleasure and satisfaction.

In developing his Theory X and Theory Y notions of management in *The Human Side of Enterprise*, McGregor leans heavily on Maslow's theory.[8] Traces of the theory are also found in Likert's *New Patterns of Management* emphasizing the participative approach to management.[9] And the influence of Maslow is to be seen in the theoretical presentation of Argyris's *Integrating the Individual and the Organization.*[10] The essential theme of these scholars is that relationships encouraging dependence, submissiveness, conformity, and imposed evaluation must give way to relationships which hold opportunity for development of trust, for independence of action, for risk taking, and for self-evaluation. The industrial humanist movement thus encourages development of greater interpersonal competency on the part of managers. Therefore, in addition to learning more about the rational approaches to management—decision theory, operations research, simulation— managers must learn to work at the "gut level" of feelings and emotions.

This is not to say that contemporary management thought abandons the ideas of authority and control in organizational relationships. It seems apparent that the trend in management thought is toward the development of more positive approaches to the motivation of man in organizational situations, with emphasis on trust and participation as vehicles for developing opportunity for self-actualization.

Yet the literature is equally clear on another point. It is that rigid and stereotyped notions of management styles belong, to borrow a phrase from John Kenneth Galbraith, in the museum of irrelevant ideas. There is no personality syndrome characteristic of all effective leaders nor a management style appropriate for all organizational situations. Flexibility is the key word. There is a time for independence and a time for control; a time for participation and a time for authority. Contrary to what some may think, flexibility in management style demands a greater competency than does a single approach. Flexibility requires the development of a broad knowledge base, the exercise of balanced judgment in matching style with situation, and careful consideration of values so that flexibility does not degenerate into opportunism.

We add a brief postscript to this discussion of motivation and management philosophy to mention another approach to the study of motivation in modern organizations—one which the reader may find particularly provocative. Our analysis of the changing mood of human motivation and management philosophy has proceeded from a psychological base. But in *The New Industrial State* Galbraith suggests in an argument that is based on economic rather than psychological grounds, that the motivation of men in organizations has changed. Briefly, he says:

> Power in economic life has over time passed from its ancient association with land to association with capital and then on, in recent time, to the composite of knowledge and skills which comprises the technostructure. Reflecting the symmetry that so conveniently characterizes reality, there have been associated shifts in the motivations to which men respond. Compulsion has an ancient association with land. Pecuniary motivation had a similar association with capital. Identification and adaptation are associated with the technostructure.[11]

Here "Technostructure" is a term coined by Galbraith to describe the organized intelligence found in the groups of highly trained specialists who provide the motive power in modern organizations. Though his analysis proceeds from a basis of economic change rather than from a consideration of psychological needs, the results are strikingly parallel. Compulsion is the motivation of authority. Pecuniary motivation is that of money. Identification and adaptation are the motivations associated with the merging of individual goals and aspirations with the organization's goals.

From whatever framework one may view contemporary management philosophy—whether from an economic, psychological, or sociological perspective—it is apparent that the concepts of trust, participation, and self-actualization are key elements in all frames of reference. Having thus briefly explored management philosophy as one of the determinants of individual behavior, we now turn to the second element of our simplified model, organizational structure.

The Effect of Structure

In contemporary society, a term frequently tossed about is "bureaucracy." Most often the context of its use will be an unfavorable one. Yet the various forms of bureaucracy found today are perhaps the most efficient means that man has found for accomplishing complex tasks.

Indeed, we might even observe that bureaucracy represents a type of innovation in human relationships. It is apparent, however, that the formal and static kind of structure described by Weber has significant limitations when measured against the demand of contemporary society. In this discussion, four such limitations, which illustrate how organizational structure has an impact on individual behavior, will be described.

Reduces Opportunity for Individual Psychological Success

One of the most critical indictments of contemporary organizational patterns is that they reduce the opportunity for individuals to achieve self-actualization. This point of view is especially prominent in the research and writings of Chris Argyris.[12] The concept is essentially this. Modern hierarchical structures are based on the principles and philosophy of scientific management—which includes such familiar ideas as chain of command, span of control, and task specialization. And, the prevalent managerial philosophy has been that man is opposed to work. Thus, a combination of restrictive managerial controls and jobs fragmented by technology and specialization act to reduce opportunities for individual challenge and self-actualization—especially at the lower levels in the hierarchy.

As a result, at some levels in our organizational structures we have so fragmented job responsibilities that employees are using only a narrow range of their talents. Faced with the frustration which comes from lack of challenge, employees may react by expending much of their energy in nonproductive activities. Expenditure of energy in these adaptive activities reduces the productive output of the organization. The cycle is thus made complete, because these types of employee behaviors convince administrators that more controls are needed.

Contributes to Organizational Inertia

Another serious criticism of contemporary organizational structures is that they contribute to inertia by reducing opportunity for change. John Gardner has pointed out the need for continued "self-renewal" at both the individual and organizational levels and has clearly explained that a readiness to grow and change is critical in contemporary society.[13] Yet those familiar with the workings of large organizations know that it is difficult to surmount the rigidity which comes with formalization of activities. One of the mechanisms of the impediment is explained by Victor Thompson.

> Hierarchical relations overemphasize the veto and underemphasize approval of innovation. Since there is no appeal from the superior's decision, a veto usually ends the matter. However, an approval will often have to go to the next higher level where it is again subject to veto. A hierarchical system always favors the status quo.[14]

Thus, communication is often inhibited in the hierarchical structure. Of course, there are other more complex concepts involved in this problem of resistance to change. We refer especially to the problem of individual status and role expectations associated with hierarchical structures. The basic idea is, however, that organizational inertia is encouraged by the "chain of command" concept inherent in contemporary patterns.

Inhibits Effective Decision Making

Today's society is one of specialization and increased interdependence, but we find it difficult to integrate specialists into hierarchical organizational patterns. In times gone past, the "boss" usually had come up through the ranks so that he knew every job under his supervision better than anyone working for him. This, of course, is no longer true. The diversity of organizational activities makes it impossible for one man to know it all. What school principal, superintendent, or college president can possess an effective command of the variety of activities found in modern educational organizations?

Galbraith emphasizes the contribution of specialization as he points out:

> The real accomplishment of modern science and technology consists of taking ordinary men, informing them narrowly and deeply and then through appropriate organization, arranging to have their knowledge combined with that of other specialized but equally ordinary men.[15]

He goes on to emphasize the need for coordination.

> Finally, following the need for this variety of specialized talent, is the need for its coordination. Talent must be brought to bear on the common purpose. More specifically, on large and small matters, information must be extracted from the various specialists, tested for its reliability and relevance, and made to yield a decision.[16]

The tasks of designing an "appropriate organization" and achieving "coordination" are the ones which are made more difficult by contemporary organizational patterns.

Thompson maintains:

> Modern bureaucracy is an adaptation of older organizational forms altered to meet the need of specialization. Modern specialization is grafted into it, but old traces of the past remain. Along with technological specialization, we find survivals of Genghis Khan and the aboriginal war chiefs. We find the latest in science and technology associated with the autocratic, monistic, hierarchical organization of a simpler time.[17]

His thesis is that in modern organizations there is a growing imbalance between ability and authority—between the right to make decisions, which is authority, and the power to do so, which is specialized ability. Through the creation of staff agencies, cabinet methods of governance, and various council and committee structures, some of the limitations outlined by

Thompson have been overcome, but a number of problems remain unresolved.

Encourages Mechanistic View of Organization

Contemporary organizational patterns encourage a mechanistic view of organizational functions. With a mechanistic perspective, little relationship is discerned among the various parts of the organization. This restricted perspective has little correspondence with the reality of organizational functions, which is that the vitality of an organization depends upon the vitality of each component.

The dysfunctional consequences of an administrator's failure to take an organic view of an organization are readily apparent. For example, the school principal who evaluates his faculty without regard to the capabilities of students or availability of teaching resources is taking a mechanistic view of his organization. The school superintendent who evaluates the effectiveness of his records division without any thought to the status of his computer and data processing division is taking a mechanistic view of his school system. The college president who feels that he can develop a strong department of psychology while neglecting to build strength in departments with which psychology may relate is taking a mechanistic view of the university. Indeed, any educational manager who makes decisions without careful reflection on the impact throughout the organization has a case of "tunnel vision" with regard to the true nature of organizations today.

What implications do these concepts of structure have for the educational manager? What points of focus and emphasis are suggested for practice? Clearly, the administrator must address himself to the challenges of (1) defining job responsibilities so that a great array of human talents are called into play, (2) creating a sensitive balance between organizational control and independence of action so that change and innovation are facilitated rather than inhibited, (3) designing organizational relationships so that maximum contribution of specialists can be realized, and (4) developing an organic perspective of organizations so that he remains vigilant to the interdependency of organizational components.

In closing this discussion, we readily admit that it is easier to recommend than it is to transform recommendation into action. At the same time, however, a more professional approach to administration begins with awareness. The writers share with other practicing educational managers the obligation of translating awareness into action.

The Impact of Group Membership

Occasionally managers fall into the habit of thinking that the most important variables related to individual behavior are those associated with the vertical relationships in line and staff charts. However, these formal relationships are only the above-surface part of the "iceburg" of organizational structure. In the words of Laurence Iannaccone:

> For centuries, some students of organization have thought that the formal organization is only what appears on the surface of organizational life and is given lip service. They have felt that beneath the formal organization, and obscured in part by it, there lies a "real" world consisting of the way things actually get done and how people truly behave in organizations.[18]

If research into organizational life has produced any finding of significance to the practicing manager, it is that peer relationships—both formal and informal—are critical variables in organizational productivity.

The study of group dynamics has produced some fruitful concepts concerning human behavior. It is not our purpose in this discussion to attempt a synopsis of the fields included in the study of group dynamics. To capsule areas such as the study of communication networks, leadership styles, attitude shaping, or group counseling would be impossible; but perhaps one or two examples will illustrate the importance of group membership on individual behavior.

One of the things known from the study of group dynamics is that every individual in an organization is a member of both formal and informal groups and that these groups can have particular impact upon his attitudes and behavior. The literature abounds with laboratory and action research studies which reveal how group pressures can affect both the quality and speed with which tasks are accomplished and how groups can influence judgment. Educational managers are in no way free from such influence. Research shows that higher levels of education provide no immunity from pressures to conform. Thus, in understanding behavior within the organization, the alert manager must remain sensitive to horizontal and diagonal relationships, the lines of which may extend outside the framework of the organization.

In the study of community and school relationships, educational managers learn to define both the overt and covert power structures in the community. A sensitivity to these structures is a valuable asset in a number of ways. Perhaps an equally attentive study of both the above-surface and the subterranean structures within the organization would also prove fruitful.

Since our emphasis in this discussion is predominantly on the group membership effect on individual attitudes and behavior, it is appropriate to digress for the purpose of outlining an interesting motivation psychology which has emerged from the study of group behavior. We refer to the "cognitive dissonance" theory proposed by Leon Festinger.[19] The core ideas of this theory are rather straightforward. Individuals are often confronted with conflicting notions or "cognitions" which do not fit well together. For example, a teacher may feel that a strike is an appropriate professional action but at the same time may feel that it is unfair to the student. It is easy to see how different group memberships can bring pressure to bear on this point of individual conflict or dissonance.

Or consider the dissonance generated for a manager who finds that the organizational chart dictates that he relate directly to another manager for whom he has an intense personal dislike, a dislike derived from an extraorganizational association. According to Festinger, these conflicts or dissonances have motivation features because the dissonance will lead to behavior designed to reduce the dissonance. The teacher may decide that a temporary sacrifice of student welfare may be necessary for the long-range welfare of other students, thus weighing in favor of the strike action. The educational manager may decide that his personal feelings are less important than the welfare of his division, or he may find ways to circumvent the formal line of relationships. Cognitive dissonance theory has proved to be of considerable utility in predicting a wide range of behavior, and a basic familiarity with the concepts involved could prove to be of value in understanding behavior as well.

A number of other variables have been researched for their effect on group performance and individual behavior. Research has included probes into (1) task variables, such as the effect of required time and task complexity; (2) structural variables, such as size of group, opportunity for interaction, and homogeneity of group talent; (3) leadership style, such as task orientation and group maintenance functions; and (4) communications, such as a network composition study of the speed of task completion and member satisfaction. This discussion is brief.Our purpose here is only to stimulate the administrator to remain sensitive to the importance of both informal and formal relationships.

The Influence of Individual Personality

The determinants of individual behavior thus far considered have been external rather than internal. However, there is another perspective—and associated psychology—which is in contrast to the three points of view previously considered. This perspective is most clearly captured in the writings of Abraham Zaleznik, who says:

> The energy and vitality that make organizations move depend upon individual initiative. Leaders with brilliant ideas and the capacity to inspire thought and action in others are the main generators of energy. The effects of their personality induce a contagion to perform that is considerably stronger in directing organizations than depersonalized systems such as interlocking committee structures or participative management. The release of individual energy and the contagion to perform occur within organizational structures. But the impulse and inspiration derive from individual personality.[20]

Zaleznik goes on to analyze man-organization interaction from a framework of Freudian psychology. His theme is that many of the problems encountered in man-organization conflict may be better understood from an internal view than from an external one. From the standpoint of Freudian psychology, the determinants of present behavior are to be found in the past experience of the individual. Zaleznik's thesis is that much dysfunctional behavior in organizations may be explained as a failure of the individual to achieve psychological maturity.

His exposition of leadership dilemmas, subordinancy relationships, status conflicts, and other organizational problems in terms of individual personality development is conceptually rich. We will explore two concepts which illustrate the importance of this idea for the educational manager.

Our first example is the problem of communication in administrative behavior. There has been significant emphasis given to the development of the ability to listen creatively and to empathize. Such an emphasis has a client-centered counseling orientation as proposed by Carl Rodgers.[21] Certainly, the manager will admit to frequent situations when listening is the appropriate administrative behavior. But as Zaleznik points out, there are also situations which call for a posture more directive in character.

> It is important for both superior and subordinate to know where one stands on issues of work or personal conflict. We usually hear that it is important to listen to the other person and understand his point of view. This is good advice as far as it goes. What gets left out to the misfortune of all concerned is the fact that competent behavior depends on the ability of the individual to know where he stands and what he would like to see happen. In particular, the authority figure may find himself tyrannized by his own vacillations. If the subordinate is confused and torn by mixed feelings, it will do him little good to find his boss is equally confused. In this sense, knowing where one stands and being prepared to take a position has a salutary effect on human relationships.[22]

Our purpose here is not to emphasize one point of view at the expense of the other. It is to reinforce the idea of flexibility which we earlier proposed in our discussion of management philosophy.

Another concept of special interest to the manager concerns the relationship of "personality orientation and executive functions." One of the significant findings of behavioral research is that there is no personality syndrome characteristic of all effective leaders. Another way of saying this is, research has suggested that effective leadership is often as much determined by situational variables as by personality variables. In his book *Management by Objectives,* George S. Odiorne makes the point clear by analogy.[23] He suggests that effective management is similar to effective acting. The successful actor, knowledgeable of his strengths and limitations, pays attention to the selection of the play so that it will be compatible with his strengths and limitations. Likewise, the manager should learn to assess his abilities so that he can achieve a harmonious and productive match of personality with function. Zaleznik illustrates the interaction between managerial personality and functions by the following diagram:

Figure 3. The Interaction of Executive Functions and Personality Orientations.[24]

Executive Functions-Organizational Requisites

		Homeostatic	Mediative	Proactive
Investment In				
Personality Orientation	Persons	1	2	3
	Persons and Tasks	2	1	3
	Ideas and Tasks	3	2	1

1-Major Performance
2-Secondary Performance
3-Avoided Performance

The interaction model of Figure 3 may be interpreted as follows. There are three types of organizational requisites or functions—homeostatic, mediative, and proactive. Homeostatic functions are passive in character and are associated with maintaining the internal stability of the organization. On the opposite end of the continuum are the proactive functions, which are those more active functions necessary for adapting the organization to its environment. These are change-oriented functions required for modifying organizational goals or the means by which the goals are achieved. Occupying an intermediate position on the continuum are the mediative functions.

Corresponding to these three types of organizational functions are three types of personality orientation. For example, the individual who is person-oriented will most probably give his major attention to the homeostatic organizational activities. In contrast, the idea- and task-oriented personality will find his major challenge and satisfaction in the proactive functions of the organization. There is a rough analogy here with some of the findings from group dynamics which suggest that two types of leaders may emerge within a group, a task-oriented leader and a group maintenance leader. The task leader keeps the group focused on goals, whereas the maintenance leader ensures the coherence and stability within the group.

The important implication of this model is that a match of personality with organizational function may be critical for both organizational productivity and individual personality development. Thus, a person-oriented individual who is thrust into an organizational position requiring a focus on tasks and goals may experience stress arising from the incompatibility of his personality and the organizational function. The same would be true of a task-oriented person finding himself in a position calling for a primary focus on interpersonal relations. These comments are not meant to suggest that individuals may be neatly and permanently categorized in disregard of growth and change in personality. They do suggest, however, that we cannot ignore personality orientation when integrating organizational and individual functions.

This particular concept also relates to a suggestion which Zaleznik makes earlier in his book. It is that the manager must develop a strong sense of identity:

> The exercise of leadership requires a strong sense of identity—knowing who one is and who one is not. The myth of the value of being an "all-around guy" is damaging to the striving of an individual to locate himself from within and then to place himself in relation to others. This active location and placement of oneself prevents the individual from being defined by others in uncongenial terms. It prevents him also from being buffeted around the sea of opinion he must live within. A sense of autonomy, separateness, or identity permits a freedom of action and thinking so necessary for leadership.
>
> Not the least significant part of achieving a sense of identity is the creative integration of one's past. There is no tailor who can convert a hayseed into a big-city boy— anymore than a dude can become a cowboy for all the hours he spends on the range. Coming to terms with being a hayseed or a dude permits the development of a unique person who goes beyond the stereotypes offered to him as models.[25]

The message is clear. Before he can hope to direct effectively the action of others, the manager must first acquire a mastery of himself.

We have hardly circumscribed the full range of concepts which are embodied in this emphasis on individual personality. But we hope that the illustrations presented do reveal the importance of individual personality in the influence of individual behavior at all levels of the organizational hierarchy.

Summary

What points of emphasis are suggested for the educational manager aspiring to develop a more commanding professional competence? Among the many concepts which may be extracted from our discussion, the following are most important.

The causes of individual behavior in organizations are multivariate. The educational manager needs to remember, therefore, that the determinants of behavior emerge from a matrix composed of management philosophy, organizational structure, group memberships, and individual personality.

As we consider the elements of this matrix, we find that contemporary research and theorizing in management philosophy indicate that the most productive relationships are those in which dependence, submissiveness, conformity, and external evaluation give way to relationships which hold opportunity for the development of trust, for independence of action, for risk taking, and for self-evaluation. The latter elements are essentials in providing organizational opportunity for the individual to achieve self-actualization.

This is not to suggest that the notions of authority and control are absent in current thought. It does mean that rigid and stereotyped ideas of administrative style must be replaced by a more flexible perspective which encourages the matching of style with situation. Such administrative flexibility requires the development of a strong interpersonal competency, and this competency derives from a broad knowledge base and a willingness to work at the "gut level" of feelings and emotions where there are few rational guides for action. A flexible managerial style demands also the development of a carefully considered value framework which prevents flexibility from degenerating into opportunism.

We have also seen that contemporary hierarchical organizational patterns may impede (1) individual self-actualization, (2) change and innovation, (3) effective use of specialists in decision making, and (4) development of an organic view of the organization. The administrator must confront the challenges of designing organizational patterns and relationships so that a greater array of human abilities are called into play, of creating a sensitive balance between control and independence so that change and innovation are facilitated, of overcoming rigid notions of relationships so that specialists are efficiently used in decision making, and of developing an organic perspective of organizations so that the interdependence of organizational components is seen.

By considering the effects of group membership on individual behavior, the manager becomes sensitive to the importance of diagonal and horizontal relationships within the organization. Individuals in the organization are members of groups, both formal and informal, whose lines of influence may extend well beyond the formal boundaries of the organization. An awareness, then, of both the overt and covert power relationships— of the above-surface and subterranean aspects of the organization—is indispensable for the manager who is interested in understanding and predicting individual behavior.

Although what we have said thus far emphasizes the importance of external forces on individual behavior, a point which should not be forgotten is that powerful internal forces for action are present in the personalities of individuals. The energy which moves organizations comes from individuals. It is not proper, therefore, to see members of an organization simply as passive elements, moving at the whim of external forces. A harmonious integration of individual and organization is more likely to emerge when careful attention is given to the interaction between individual personal orientation and the various organizational tasks.

DISCUSSION QUESTIONS/LEARNING ACTIVITIES

1. To what extent is behavior "determined?" What factors, other than those outlined in this chapter, may be "determinants" of behavior?

2. There is much discussion in business and industrial literature about the merits of "job enlargement." What does this mean and what form has it taken in companies? Are there implications for education?

3. Educational managers sometimes label an ineffective colleague as "incompetent." To what extent may such incompetence really be a mismatch of the person and the job?

4. We have taken the position that educational managers must be flexible in their style and artistic in application of concepts. Do you believe this is in conflict with the notion that administrators have basic style inclinations?

5. Develop a rating form that contains statements of philosophical assumptions. Administer this rating form to educational managers you know and compare their responses with your assessment of their managerial attitudes.

6. Many management concepts revolve around Maslow's hierarchy of needs. Conduct a literature search to see if you can discover any criticism or contrasting point of view on his theory.

Notes

1. Bernard M. Bass, *Organizational Psychology* (Boston: Allyn and Bacon, 1965).

2. Victor Thompson, *Modern Organizations* (New York: Alfred A. Knopf, 1961).

3. William G. Scott, *Organization Theory: A Behavioral Analysis for Management* (Homewood, Ill: Richard D. Irwin, 1967).

4. J. G. March (ed.), *Handbook of Organizations* (Chicago: Rand McNally, 1965).

5. Frederick Winslow Taylor, *Scientific Management* (New York: Harper & Row, 1947).

6. Scott, *Organization Theory,* p. 43.

7. Abraham H. Maslow, *Motivation and Personality* (New York: Harper and Brothers, 1954).

8. Douglas McGregor, *The Human Side of Enterprise* (New York: McGraw-Hill, 1960).

9. Rensis Likert, *New Patterns of Management* (New York: McGraw-Hill, 1961).

10. Chris Argyris, *Integrating the Individual and the Organization* (New York: John Wiley and Sons, 1964).

11. John Kenneth Galbraith, *The New Industrial State* (Boston: Houghton Mifflin Co., 1967), p. 143.

12. Argyris, *Integrating the Individual and the Organization.*

13. John Gardner, *Self-Renewal* (New York: Harper & Row, 1964).

14. Thompson, *Modern Organizations,* p. 61.

15. Galbraith, *The New Industrial State,* p. 62.

16. *Ibid.,* p. 63.

17. Thompson, *Modern Organizations,* p. 5.

18. Laurence Iannaccone, "An Approach to the Informal Organization of the School," *Behavioral Science and Educational Administration: The Sixty-third Yearbook of the National Society for*

　　the Study of Education, Part II, Daniel E. Griffiths, (ed.), (Chicago: University of Chicago Press, 1964). p. 223.

19. Leon Festinger, *Theory of Cognitive Dissonance* (Evanston, Ill.: Peterson and Co., 1957).

20. Abraham Zaleznik, *Human Dilemmas of Leadership* (New York: Harper & Row, 1966), pp. 3-4.

21. Carl Rogers, *Client Centered Therapy* (New York: Houghton Mifflin, 1951).

22. Zaleznik, *Leadership*, p. 68.

23. George S. Odiorne, *Management by Objectives* (New York: Pitman, 1965).

24. Zaleznik, *Leadership,* p. 191.

25. *Ibid.,* pp. 41-42.

3
Managing Change in Education

*Is anyone afraid of change? Why, what can be done
without change? What is more pleasing or more
suitable to universal nature? Can you take a bath
unless the wood undergoes a change? Can you be
nourished, unless your food undergoes a change?
Do you not then see that for yourself also change
is the same, and equally necessary for the universal
nature?*

Marcus Aurelius, *Meditations*

Of all human institutions, there are none more important in their
influence than schools and colleges. Yet, schools and colleges
suffer from massive organizational inertia and yield slowly to
change. They do change, but the change is frequently quantitative
rather than qualitative. They get bigger but not always better.

The brick walls that mark the boundaries of some vested-
interest groups have been barriers to the educational manager
aspiring to introduce additional flexibility in curriculum, to
nurture some interest in learning technology, or to encourage a
risk-taking venture in educational programming. Some
organizational structures and processes in schools and colleges
have roots that defy the most powerful educational dynamite,
administrative bulldozing, and budgetary poisoning.

Forces acting to produce change in our schools and colleges are
everywhere visible. Colleges have emerged from a period of
student unrest and rapid growth only to enter a period of
stabilized enrollments, which may offer a greater morale crisis
than the events of the 60s. Many school systems are caught up in
the throes of social and political upheaval associated with court
decisions on busing and other issues.

Change phenomena have not gone without attention in
American education. Paul Mort and other observers of the
American education scene have been puzzled as to why new

practices could come so quickly to other fields, especially agriculture and medicine, and yet emerge so slowly in education.[1] Some research, particularly that of Mort and Cornell, suggested that change might be associated with the cost-quality relationship in education—the higher the per student expenditure the more likely a system or institution would be to foster innovation.[2] Subsequent study revealed, however, that the relationship was not so simple and that educational leadership, in both style and status, was closely allied to the change process.[3]

The challenge of change continues to receive wide attention in both the professional and public literature. In a chapter of the book *The Planning of Change,* George S. Counts remarked that "as our feet tread the earth of a new world our heads continue to dwell in a world that is gone."[4] And in his best-seller *Future Shock,* Alvin Toffler has a chapter entitled "Education in the Future Tense" in which he says:

> The rapid obsolescence of knowledge and the extension of life span make it clear that the skills learned in youth are unlikely to remain relevant by the time old age arrives. Super industrial education must therefore make provision for life long education on a plug-in/plug-out basis.[5]

And this same theme was echoed by Jerome Bruner in a paper entitled "The Continuity of Learning" when he urged that:

> The process of education (whether in established schools or by other means) be conceived not just as a preparation but as a form of enablement selectively available throughout the life cycle."[6]

Thus the most basic change force at work is a way of thinking about the educational process itself.

What are the implications for the educational manager? For one thing, educational managers should be one group of professionals who by aptitude and attitude infuse our schools and colleges with a renewing spirit. But how many educational managers can do that? Coming out of a decade of rapid growth, some of them have found it easy to associate simple quantitative activity—growth in faculty, budgets, buildings, enrollments—

with educational progress and quality. Some have been less frequently educational leaders—rule breakers and value creators—and more frequently midwives who assist schools and colleges to move in directions already determined.

The task of bringing about intelligent change presents a challenge of both a conceptual and applied character. To talk of change is not the same as effecting change. If we are to be effective change agents, we must master those social-behavioral concepts that help us understand the change process and then we must apply them artistically.

The story is told that Mark Twain was once consulted on how to handle the German submarine menace in World War I. He is reported to have said that "the solution is simple; all you have to do is boil the ocean." But those of a more practical inclination asked how this was to be accomplished. "Well," said Twain, "I thought up the solution. You have to figure out how to implement it." Unfortunately, educational managers not only bear the responsibility of finding solutions to problems but also carry the responsibility for implementation. Many attempted changes have met disastrous ends not because of unhealthy intent but because of the inadequate methods used to carry out that intent. In brief, then, we want to explore those concepts which help us understand organizational change processes, and then we will talk about the artistry needed to apply them.

Because the determinants of individual behavior in educational organizations are complex, it is not sufficient to approach a study of the processes of change solely from an individual or psychological perspective. To do so fails to recognize the complexity of the structural and role relationships that constitute the social-organizational system in which we work. Neither can we afford to look at organizational change by committing a sociological fallacy—that is, to assume that change can be effected by simple adjustment of structure and role. We wish to emphasize that resistance to educational change can be associated with both personal and structural variables. We also concern ourselves with one other variable, a knowledge variable, that may help us understand why change comes so slowly to education as compared to other professions.

Identification of Resistance Points

Individual Variables

It is surprising how much change can be generated by the three-letter word "why." Small children insist on frequent application of the word, but its use grows less frequent with age, perhaps because our basic curiosity is successfully smothered by our proclivity for convention. Here's an illustration that reveals how wedded we can become to the status quo.

The story is told that in World War II, the British made use of an antique artillery piece with a history reaching back to the Boer War. Following the fall of France, these guns served as useful interim units in coast defense. Not satisfied with the performance of the gun, however, the British determined to increase its firing rate. An efficiency expert was called upon to examine the firing procedure and to outline ways by which the firing rate might be improved. His curiosity was provoked by the performance of the five-man gun crew at work, and he took some slow motion film of the men at work in the loading, aiming, and firing routine. A close examination of the activity of each man revealed that just prior to firing, two of the five men ceased all activity and came to attention for an interval that extended through the firing of the gun. Puzzled by this apparently odd behavior, he consulted an equally venerable colonel of artillary, showed him the film, emphasizing this peculiar behavior. After seeing the film again, the old colonel resolved the mysterious behavior by suggesting that these two men were "holding the horses"—a behavior pattern extending from the time when these guns had been pulled by horses rather than trucks.

The illustration emphasizes how we resist the pain of change by continuing—even in the face of an altered environment—familiar behavior patterns. This story also illustrates that a little effort spent on the cultivation of curiosity can go a long way toward the successful introduction of change. We are still holding on to a number of imaginary academic horses in our schools and colleges.

Any educational manager could provide a host of illustrations—and without looking behind his own area of responsibility. Educators are at times subject to the same rigor mortis that afflicts many professions—a reverence for routine, a parochial view of problems, an aversion to adventure, and an abiding affection for the status quo.

The reason for this lack of openness and receptivity to change is not so complicated, but it is a little peculiar when one thinks about the setting. In education, we pride ourselves on that noble-sounding goal, "search for truth." For some reason, however, we are more able to discern the truth outside our own organizations. Why is this? Perhaps it is because curiosity has a tendency to draw us into situations that involve conflict and confrontation. History is replete with illustrations to confirm the cruel ways in which we often deal with those who dare to meddle with the status quo. To engage issues, therefore, that bring us into contact with those having differing points of view and conviction calls for a good deal of personal strength and identity. It calls for educational managers who can sustain threats to their egos and a flexing of their values. As Eric Hoffer points out in *The Ordeal of Change,* "every radical adjustment is a crisis in self-esteem; we undergo a test, we have to prove ourselves. It needs inordinate self-confidence to face drastic change without inner trembling."[7]
success and reward but where there is little interaction with the larger organization and the social context of which it is a part. Some of us have abdicated our leadership responsibility to groups, which may be inherently more conservative. And some of us have forgotten that few great and noble events in the history of man and of professions have occurred without personal risk.

But even if we are successful in cultivating curiosity and managing conflict there is at least one other resistance force at work. It is a basic anxiety over the unknown, an anxiety that affects everyone, great or small, learned or ignorant. What we do not know or understand we fear. There is a host of research evidence—on everything from pajama making to instructional technology—that full communication and involvement of individuals in the change process tend to enhance the effectiveness of change. But we don't need a flurry of footnotes to the social-psychological literature to confirm that communication and involvement are important.

Much of the time, we choose to ignore this notion. The landscape of history is littered with the skeletons of good ideas smothered by fear—not because the idea was not a good one, but because someone did not take the time to involve those concerned and to communicate all that was involved in the change. Curiosity, confrontation, communication—we must utilize all three in order to overcome personal resistance to change.

Structural Variables

To nurture in our educational institutions those conditions that foster change, we will be only partly successful if we content ourselves with knowing that change is impeded by personal points of resistance. Schools and colleges are "organized" enterprises, and the geometry of organizations is principally a straight-line geometry. What are some of the structural properties of organizations that militate against change processes?

A first and major point of structural resistance is that educational institutions are at least partially conservative in purpose. One of their major purposes is that of preserving and transmitting the cultural heritage. This process gets a little stressful if that heritage is constantly being pulled up by the roots.

A second kind of structural impediment is the way in which educational institutions are organized. The vested interests of some departments and units form a surface that can resist the penetration of any change projectile. In educational organizations it is far easier to oppose change than facilitate it. Each faculty group and administrator has a veto response; such veto responses are a negative feedback that can prevent the implementation of major variations in policy and practice. If, for example, the implementation of a new program promises to reduce or even rearrange students or faculty, then all kinds of resistance can be expected. This is not a phenomenon restricted to educational organizations; but educational organizations are impeded in change by other complicating factors as well, one of which is the manner in which we make decisions.

Educational decision processes can involve considerable agony. School and college faculties often insist on involvement in the decision processes; collegial governance patterns still provide the model, even though, as we point out in the chapter on "Decision Processes," that decision style should be adapted to decision type. But massive and extended deliberation by various faculty and administrative groups can constitute an oppression of structure and process.

The procedures that we properly establish to protect the quality of our decision making have also the potential for impeding those changes we would like to have occur. Good men and good ideas can grow weary under continual explanation and reconsideration. The clear, simple ideas that go into our decision system can come out dull and complicated as adjustments and modifications are made to satisfy criticism. To design decision processes that will filter out weak ideas but facilitate the translation of good ideas into action requires true managerial artistry.

One final point needs emphasis as we talk about the structural properties that impede change. Reward structures in education—personal and institutional—generally do not encourage innovation and change. In elementary and secondary schools, the salary schedule is most likely to depend upon such easily recognized variables as experience and educational level rather than merit considerations. That one is a truly innovative teacher is not likely to be recognized in the paycheck. And in higher education, the reward structure rests for the most part within the discipline or department. A person's colleagues are not likely to get very excited over his promotion potential if he is the prime advocate for an academic program that cuts into the territorial rights of his discipline or in any other way threatens the welfare of the discipline.

From an institutional point of view, the reinforcement character of the external forces that act on our educational institutions tends to be more negative toward change than positive. Instead of being provided incentives for exciting programming and effective management, educational organizations are apt to be given policy guidelines on personnel workload and financial management. However, governing and legislative groups can be an important influence in encouraging change within educational organizations by rewarding institutions that do a good job instead of setting up punitive systems.

Knowledge Variables

Resistance to change in educational organizations can thus emerge from both personal and structural sources. But there is yet another characteristic of education having an important influence on the pace of change. It is related to the knowledge foundation upon which the profession is built. For example, dramatic developments in agricultural production and health care quality are based heavily upon basic research in the natural and physical sciences. Both research and evaluation are rendered more certain by the relatively precise measurements and absence of value concerns over method in these sciences. One can more easily conduct an experiment with corn or bacteria than with students. The social and behavioral sciences that form an important part of our knowledge foundation in education do not yet permit the same degree of preciseness that can be found in the physical and natural sciences.

Despite this problem, we have begun to pay more attention to the scientific bases of our profession in recent years. Moreover, this seems to be true in all fields—teaching, administration, counseling. We are attempting to be more rigorous in our search for concepts and relationships. The fact remains, however, that even some of our best research is often equivocal; nothing is more prevalent than the "no significant difference" syndrome in education. Part of our failure to detect generalized relationships is due to the simplicity of our research. In too many cases, we continue to search for the best method of teaching subject A or subject B, oblivious to many other interacting variables of student history, personality, and learning style.

Moreover, as Provus has noted, our models for research and evaluation in education have been frequently patterned after the experimental models of the sciences.[8] He suggests that these may not be altogether sufficient. For example, the administration of an educational treatment—method of teaching, style of management, approach to counseling—is not quite as simple as administering so many pounds of fertilizer to a corn plot or administering a dosage of medicine to a patient. Provus points out that educational evaluation needs to address itself not only to outputs but also to whether the treatment itself was properly administered.

We may expect the quality of educational research and evaluation to improve and to provide us with a more stable scientific knowledge base upon which to base change. However, this does not mean that we do not have a good set of concepts with which to work now. Indeed, we continue to ignore in educational practice much that is currently known. For example, research on the transfer of learning is largely ignored. In the face of research findings to the contrary, many faculty in public schools and more in higher education still subscribe to the notion that the mind is a series of "faculties" to be exercised.

Learning research in the area of "reinforcement" suggests that behavior can be changed effectively through the application of reinforcements. Yet papers that are carefully written by students may never be returned with any kind of reinforcement, positive or negative. We continue to give course grades based on a single examination or test, even though measurement theory and research indicate that error can be extradordinarily high when there is only a single sampling of performance.

In counseling, we continue to make decisions about individuals as though our measurement instruments were precise intellectual and personal calipers, even though measurement research emphasizes the dependence of raw scores not only upon student performance but upon the construction of the instrument and the environment in which it was administered. And a similar simplicity afflicts some educational managers who hold to the notion that one management style is invariably more effective than another, even though research indicates that style effectiveness is related to both task and group variables.

The following observation by Arthur Chickering, orginally directed to higher education professionals, generalizes to all educational levels.

> Education problems are outrunning solutions, not so much
> for lack of relevant principles, and not because useful steps
> are obscure, but because implementation is occurring at a
> snail's pace, because basic concepts are disdained.[9]

Thus, educational change is slow to come, not only because
research and evaluation need additional precision but because we
ignore much that we already know.

Strategies for Renewal

Schools and colleges are organized for defensive concession.
Conventional practices may be temporarily altered, but it's
difficult to effect a permanent change. If we are to infuse our
educational institutions with a spirit of renewal, we need to
concentrate not only on knowledge but on performance as well.
Thus, there may be some merit in briefly examining elements of
change strategies to see how these elements may be artistically
applied.

Relevant Versus Significant Change

First, it may be important to note that change is not a process to
be worshipped. Some educational managers find themselves
caught up in the "change ethic" and become indiscriminate in
their selection of policies and processes that need renewal. Not all
change will produce positive outcomes, and it is advisable to
pay attention to the character and possible results of change,
so that we can identify those changes that are both relevant
and significant.

As an example, the administrative council of a medium-size
college exhausted its energies on a proposal which was probably
relevant but hardly significant. The debate centered around the
design appearing on the parking decal affixed to the rear bumper
of all cars parked on the campus. The full commitment and
energy of a few members were spent in trying to convince their
colleagues that the appearance of the university mascot on the
parking decal did not give a sufficiently scholarly image.
Meanwhile, a host of other policy matters—conflicts over tenure

and promotion processes, curricular and program matters, fiscal decisions—rested quietly backstage while this relatively unimportant matter occupied the council.

Modes of Behavior Modification

The point of the previous illustration is that the educational manager must first select those change proposals that are significant to the life and vitality of his organization. Another concept useful in building change strategies concerns the identification of those changes in which involvement of other people is essential and those in which it may be more appropriate to change the environment and allow attitudes to follow.

In recent years, it has become customary to sensitize all educational managers to the importance of involvement in bringing about effective change. In the earlier discussion on personal variables and change, we referred to the importance of involvement. The educational manager who elects to ignore the importance of full communication and modes of involvement in effecting change does so at considerable personal and organizational risk. Thus, an elementary principal who summarily decided that the opening hour for his elementary school should be changed from 8:00 a.m. to 8:30 a.m., failed to anticipate the furor of the many working parents residing in the school community. After a week of verbal bombardment plus the promise of more vigorous resistance, the principal decided that he and his faculty could manage to open at 8:00 a.m. The most popular exhortation to the educational manager today is the one that contains frequent references to communication and involvement. However, some changes may require more courageous acts of leadership. In an article provocatively titled, "Human Beings Are Not Very Easy To Change After All," Amitai Etzioni, prominent sociologist and organizational scholar, suggested that:

> What is becoming increasingly apparent is that to solve social problems by changing people is more expensive and usually less productive than approaches that accept people as they are and seek to mend not them but the circumstances around them.[10]

Citing a variety of attempts in which educational processes had sought to change our habits in such areas as smoking, automobile safety, drug abuse, Eztioni concludes that:

> The contention that personal growth and societal changes are much harder to come by than we had assumed, especially via one version or another of the educationist-enlightenment approach, is not a joyful message, but one whose full implications we must learn to accept before we can devise more effective social programs.[11]

The reader searching for a more broadly based example of this approach to processes can find a highly visible example in the area of public policy and mass attitudes. Writing about public policy in the sensitive and controversial area of civil rights, political scientist Thomas Dye analyzes opinion data over an extended time period and comes to the conclusion that "Mass opinion toward civil rights has generally followed public policy, and not led it. Mass opinion did not oppose legally segregated schools until after elites had declared national policy in Brown vs. Topeka."[12]

Similarly, in regard to educational change processes, it may be more productive to change the environment and then allow attitudes to follow, rather than to wait for change in attitude to produce the change in environment.

An illustration may help to clarify this point. Several years ago, a large university was considering the introduction of an "early semester plan" in which the fall term would end before Christmas and the spring term in early May. A three week period in May was to be set aside for an intensive presummer session in which a student might concentrate on a single course. The college of education had been offering such three-week intensive courses for years, but skeptics from other colleges were convinced that nothing good could come from this arrangement. Nevertheless, the new calendar was adopted, and a small number of faculty adventurers from other colleges were enticed to offer one or two courses in the new three-week term. Their report of success and excitement in working with students in this kind of setting was so contagious that the following year a large number of other faculty began to offer courses. The modular arrangement has become so popular that now those faculty who fought the concept most vigorously are suggesting that perhaps it should be introduced during the regular term so that students would not take four simultaneous courses, but four modular courses in sequence.

Readiness and Timing

As we think about strategies for change, one other concept from the psychology of learning and child development begs our attention—the concept of readiness. Many of us can still remember times when our small children took a little longer to master skills than we felt was appropriate. Learning to ride a bike simply did not result from all the coaching and encouragement that we could give. But one day, when the child was ready— and not necessarily according to the schedule of our expectation—he exploded into the neighborhood, riding the bike as though he had been doing for years. We believe that this concept transfers to organizational life.

Anyone who has been in schools or colleges for an extended period knows that having a really fine idea and believing in it does not ipso facto ensure its acceptance and implementation. If one is riding the crest of reform, the idea may take root and blossom overnight. On the other hand, the state of organizational readiness may mean that the idea will need to be tended with a good deal of patience. The incubation period for some really fine ideas may run into years. On one university campus, the director of the evening division quietly nurtured a set of people and programs in continuing education for three or four years before the major leadership of the university recognized the vitality of what he had been doing all along. That this university now has a fine program of continuing education is a tribute to the vision and patience of this educational manager.

Summary

Change and Stability? Patience and Agressiveness? Involvement and Action? Are there any conceptual anchors to which the educational manager might tie his practice? We have tried to point out some of them and to indicate that their application requires a sense of artistry.

The educational manager should not underestimate his potential for initiating change. He has at his discretion some of the most powerful controls over the change process. For example, one of the most promising vehicles for the introduction of change rests in the appointment process. If properly selected, new people bring new ideas, new vitality, and new energy. Thus, educational managers can take a giant step toward organizational renewal by employing professionals who are open and curious.

Another instrument of change rests with structural relationships. When ideas get captured in committees, educational managers can often reduce hierarchy, sidestep hurdles, and loosen authority structures.

Finally, we should remember that organizational change is linked to individual change. We live in organizations, but the impulse and inspiration for what happens to these organizations derive from individual personality. Men and women who have ideas and commitment and who can inspire both thought and action in others are the power source for our schools and colleges. The challenges facing our schools and colleges will lead some of them to greatness and some to oblivion. The choice is not an organizational choice. It is an individual choice. The history of our schools and colleges will record the measure of our devotion to a renewing spirit, for that history resolves into personal biography.

DISCUSSION QUESTIONS/LEARNING ACTIVITIES

1. To what extent are educators inclined to introduce change without an adequate basis for evaluating the effectiveness of the new idea or practice—or the one it is to replace?

2. Co-option, not rejection, has been identified by one writer as the real barrier to change in education. What does he mean by this?

3. What are the more significant changes that have occurred in American education over the past 100 years? From a historical context, did these changes emerge as a result of professional initiative or forces largely external to the profession?

4. Performance contracting was once hailed as a significant change mechanism in education. Conduct a search of the literature to assess the impact of this practice.

5. Develop a case study report of a successful change action in a school or college. Identify the factors that contributed to the successful implementation of this change action.

6. Identify a change in policy, practice, or structure that was initiated against majority feeling but was eventually accepted. What risks did the responsible educational manager take and what factors contributed to the eventual acceptance of the change?

NOTES

1. Paul R. Mort, "Educational Adaptability," in Donald H. Ross (ed.), *Administration for Adaptability* (New York: Metropolitan School Study Council, 1958).

2. Paul R. Mort and Francis G. Cornell, *American Schools in Transition* (New York: Teachers College, Columbia University, 1941).

3. Richard O. Carlson, *Adoption of Educational Innovations* (Eugene, Ore.: The Center for the Advanced Study of Educational Administration, University of Oregon, 1965).

4. George S. Counts, "The Impact of Technological Change," in *The Planning of Change,* Warren G. Bennis and others (eds.), (New York: Holt, Rinehart and Winston, 1961), p. 21.

5. Alvin Toffler, *Future Shock* (New York: Random House, 1970), p. 361.

6. Jerome S. Bruner, "On the Continuity of Learning," *Saturday Review of Education,* March 1973, p. 23.

7. Eric Hoffer, *The Ordeal of Change* (New York: Harper & Row, 1963) p. 3.

8. Malcolm Provus, *Discrepancy Evaluation* (Berkeley: McCutchan, 1971).

9. Arthur Chickering, *Education and Identity* (San Francisco: Jossey Bass, 1969), p. 280.

10. Amitai Etzioni, "Human Beings Are Not Very Easy To Change After All," *Saturday Review,* June 3, 1972, pp. 45-46.

11. *Ibid.,* p. 47.

12. Thomas R. Dye, *Understanding Public Policy* (Englewood Cliffs, N.J.: Prentice-Hall, 1972), p. 66.

4
Developing Managerial Theory

*We make decisions on the basis of generalizations
and assumptions (hidden or explicit) and, in so
doing we act in terms of a theory. If this is done
without full awareness, difficulty is not so much with
the decision as with the basis for it (the theory).
Consider, for instance, the superintendent who may
observe that certain desirable curriculum
improvements came about in a neighboring district
soon after publication of a new course of study; he
may then spend a summer writing a course of study
for his district, publish it, and expect curriculum
improvements to follow. Or consider the principal
who, as a classroom teacher, "always did what he
was told" and also felt that he was successful in that
role; he may now believe that teachers who are not
in agreement with him cannot be doing anything
of much value.*

Arthur P. Coladarci and Jacob W. Getzels,
The Use of Theory in Educational Administration

In Chapter 1 it was noted that some educational managers
operate on a day-to-day basis instead of planning, executing, and
evaluating with continuity, consciousness, and direction.
Substantiation for such a charge can be established quite easily by
studying the log of educational managers, by observing the
manner in which daily and weekly decisions are made, and even
by listening to educational managers "talk shop." Heard
frequently in response to the inevitable question of "How are
things going?" are comments such as, "I'm a classic case of the
administrative concept of greasing the squeaky wheel," or
"Tomorrow we're going to get organized," or "Starting next week
we're moving from a crisis by the day to crisis by the week," or "I
must be a big wheel because I am constantly going around in
circles."

Commonplace also are wall plaques and desk signs in their offices which exhort educational managers to "Think" or "Plan Ahead" but which, by intent, indicate that the opposite was employed in designing the message. Often they are reflections of the educational manager's attempt to be humorous about what he inwardly regards as a serious problem and a shortcoming on his part.

Many factors undoubtedly contribute to this situation. For example, the workload of the typical educational manager has increased at an exponential rate. There are increased pressures and expectations from within, such as changing codes of student behavior and increased teacher militancy. There are increased pressures from without, such as closer scrutiny and increased expectations (accountability) by local, state, and national governmental agencies, constantly changing and ever-increasing requirements by accrediting and regulatory bodies, rebelling taxpayers, and the "invasion" by the courts into matters formerly thought to be the sole province of education.

A contributing factor, also, is that most educational institutions are now thoroughly interwoven into the overall fabric of American society, and thus are integral parts of many of society's problems—drug abuse, racial friction, increased permissiveness of youth and adults, and inflation, just to mention a few. Schools and colleges are obviously affected, as are their administrators, by the sociological phenomenon of mobility, which in recent years has brought "a different kind of people" into formerly quiet and stable communities, or large numbers of poorly educated and unskilled persons from rural areas to urban settings.

Educational institutions and their managers are caught up in these and other problems because schools are obligated to be responsive to both the needs of individuals and their communities and, by inference at least, obligated to help solve their problems. But educational institutions have addressed themselves to these and other problems in vastly different ways—and with widely differing degrees of effectiveness. Some colleges and schools have entered into these new arenas of action enthusiastically, while others have been "dragged in kicking and screaming."

What roles should educational organizations play in solving these problems? How and by whom is the answer to this question determined? We suggest that the philosophical stance of the educational manager has a lot to do with it. If the educational manager decides to enter into these arenas, then a major factor in determining his effectiveness as leader and manager will be his philosophical stance. This in no way discounts the need and importance of other managerial and leadership skills.

No one promised educational managers that their jobs would be easy. The proliferation of problems, their increased complexity, and their obvious relationship to the purposes and goals of education (such problems are, in many instances, the results of educational goals not having been achieved) have caused some educational managers to return to classroom teaching. Others have chosen early retirement. Still others have stayed in the battle, but with little enthusiasm and scarcely with a feeling of success. But many educational managers are acting in accordance with the advice given by Warren Barr Knox, writing in the *Eye of the Hurricane,* an aptly named book of observations on creative educational administration. Knox suggests that:

> It is essential that we look affirmatively upon those situations which appear to be totally negative. Of course they are bothersome, time-consuming, and costly expenders of energy, but we should welcome the opportunity to try to resolve problems, to right wrongs, to heal wounds, and to correct misunderstandings—to practice our chosen art. On the other hand, most boards and students and faculty will make allowances for inaction, tolerate negativism, make exceptions for languishing leadership, understand the administrative maxim that tomorrow will take care of itself for about as long as it takes to get to tomorrow. Why not trade a tomorrow's worth of anguish for five minutes in the eye of the hurricane?[1]

Although it may sometimes be argued that theory and philosophy are impractical, the reverse proposition has more credence, especially when one recognizes that *all action taken* reflects some kind of underlying belief, some kind of value orientation, and some kind of philosophical underpinning, even though they may be poorly defined, internally inconsistent or even subconscious.

In the following statement, E. Grady Bogue contends that a good theory has the essential characteristic of being workable.

> . . . a good theory is one which has logical coherence, which is comprehensive, which is parsimonious, and which is workable—the last criterion is one which is of real interest to the practicing administrator, for the practitioner is sometimes inclined to view theory as being rather impractical, whereas a good theory will be imminently practical and, therefore, of real utility to him in his every day work.[2]

The "practical value" of theory, indeed the interdependence of theory and practice, is well explained by Graff, Street, Kimbrough and Dykes:

> Viewed from an organismic context, it is apparent that theory and practice in school administration are interrelated elements in the on-going processes of administration. As these elements come into proper relationship, they increase in meaning and importance. Obviously, practice without the directing influence of theory leads to anarchy and a general breakdown of the administrative enterprise, or into dictatorship with its lack of personal freedom. Obviously, also, people cannot work together in a cooperative enterprise unless there is a degree of common agreement as to theory and values.[3]

There is a great need for the educational manager to develop a philosophical and theoretical underpinning—a way for him to put into perspective and to conceptualize problems, organizational objectives, and alternative operational styles. In the remaining portions of this chapter we suggest a process by which the educational manager might develop a workable philosophical base to guide his operational style. We then identify several advantages the educational manager can expect when such a plan guides his work. The chapter concludes with a warning to educational managers about the assaults commonly made against their philosophical and theoretical underpinnings.

Developing a Theory
to Guide Operation and Management

An educational manager does not "shop" for a theory to guide his operation as he might shop for a suit of clothes, a house, or a car. Neither does he "select" one during formal preparation for the position, although much of what he learns while preparing for a managerial role ultimately finds its way into the philosophical base that he finally adopts. More often an educational manager develops a conscious and describable theory to underlie his role by combining study (covering both scholarly writings in the field and findings from research) with a serious reflection of his experiences on a job.

The educational manager may develop a theoretical base for his role by one of several processes. The process described below is sound, reliable, and adaptable to varying circumstances and types of educational settings. But first we need to define the word "theory." A definition that supports the contention that a theory is to be *developed* by the manager rather than *adopted* by him is offered by Robert L. Saunders, Ray C. Phillips, and Harold T. Johnson:

> Theory is a set of assumptions or generalizations supported by related philosophical assumptions and scientific principles. These assumptions or generalizations serve as a basis for projecting hypotheses which suggest a course of action. The hypotheses are then subjected to scientific investigation. The findings of this scientific investigation are evaluated in order to validate new scientific principles and philosophical assumptions.[4]

Thus, theory as defined above, is operational in nature. These authors view theory as a process from which content is derived and which contains five sequential components: (1) philosophical assumptions and scientific principles, (2) theoretical assumptions or generalizations, (3) hypotheses, usually stated as "if-then" situations, (4) scientific investigation-action, and (5) testing-evaluation.[5]

These steps are cyclical and never-ending. Each step interlocks with the ones which precede and follow it, and the theorizing process continues as long as the manager or administrator conscientiously attempts to maintain it in his operational style. Figure 4, reprinted from the book by Saunders, Phillips, and Johnson, illustrates the process quite well and shows both the interdependence of these steps and the cyclical nature of the theory process. Especially appropriate to the purpose of this chapter is the *movement* inherent in the process; from *thinking* to *acting* and from *known knowledge* to *new knowledge*.

Figure 4. Steps in the Theory Process

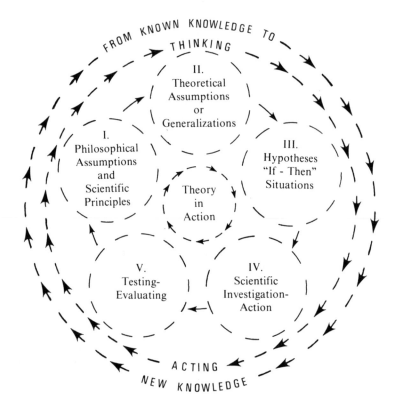

The educational manager, then, *develops* the content of his own theory rather than adopting it from an authority or from a colleague who seems to be successful and whose style he admires.

But workable theories cannot be developed well in a vacuum; that is, without the benefit of on-the-job experience. On the other hand, a manager should not place total reliance on experience and ignore the knowledge base that is fundamental to a profession.

Purposes and Uses of Theory

The educational manager performs his role more effectively with a theoretical grounding than he does without one. There are several advantages a theoretically-grounded educational manager has over his counterpart who operates independently of conscious, theoretical considerations.

Theory Lends Purpose and Direction to Operational Management

According to the definition cited above, a theory requires that the educational manager be conscious of certain philosophical assumptions and scientific principles which he holds to be true and which lead him to formulate or project certain hypotheses which he subsequently submits to examination. These steps, in and of themselves, constitute a direction or course of action. Following these steps precludes any "short circuiting" of the interdependent sequences involved in the process.

The conscious use of theory enables the educational manager to decide upon a course of action *which he believes* to be consistent with his *beliefs* about various factors involved in making a decision, such as his beliefs about people, processes and objectives. He then formulates certain hypotheses which he subsequently tests. The test may substantiate his beliefs, or it may not. Depending on the outcome, the educational manager then has a basis for whatever subsequent course of action he decides to employ. This is a very different style of operation from the one which involves "horseback" judgments and decisions.

Theory Provides Both a Justification and Explanation for Action Taken

Sometimes the most difficult, and often the most embarrassing, questions that educational administrators encounter are *why* a particular course of action was taken, *why* a particular decision was made, or *why* a particular policy was adopted. Answers such as "This is what most other institutions are doing," or "This is what the authorities in the field say should be done," are rarely satisfactory to the serious-minded questioner and never complimentary to the educational manager or his profession. Much more defensible are answers such as "This course of action was consistent with my beliefs (about people, about the hierarchy of objectives) and seemed to hold greater promise for an effective solution to this problem than did other courses of action which were considered but rejected," and "This course of action seemed to be warranted in view of similar experiences in the past which were found, through careful evaluation, to work satisfactorily," Thus the theory process imposes upon the practitioner a certain discipline and a systematic procedure.

Theory Promotes Consistency in Behavior

The educational manager who remains conscious of his theoretical bases and who remains true to them in his day-to-day operations is in a much better position to maintain a consistent style of operation. His behavior, his decision-making style, and even the manner with which he handles subjective factors and information are less likely to be conflicting, capricious, and arbitrary, because he is operating from the same frame of reference, the same set of values, and the same set of scientific facts.

Arliss L. Roaden supports this thesis when he states that:

> Unless all of one's experiences throughout life are to be trial and error, a complete holocaust of happenstance from one moment to the next, then it must be concluded that the individual is able to provide some organization and direction for his experiences. The normal purposive drives of seeking affection, food, survival, sex, etc. are inadequate to provide intelligent direction throughout life. It is the process of purposive organization and direction that is attributed to theory.[6]

Theory Helps Resist Miscellaneous Behavior

Closely related to the above point is the pressure constantly placed on the educational manager to make quick decisions, to react instantaneously to pressurized situations, and to respond hourly to a wide array of problem situations. How does the educational manager develop a way to make quick decisions which yield fruitful results or, for that matter, to decide when decisions must be made quickly and which ones can and should wait? Similarly, how does he determine priorities, the tasks which deserve his first and foremost attention?

Our contention is, again, that he is more likely to make wise decisions about these and other similar matters if he approaches them with a perspective; a frame of reference which, in effect, has helped him to make some decisions and to anticipate the need to make others. Operating from a reference frame or a theory enables him to evaluate and record similar problem situations and to be conscious of how they were handled and how effective they proved to be. This is step five of the theory process— evaluation. Having a deeply ingrained set of values and having acquired the ability to quickly collate the essential components of a particular problem into this frame of reference should reduce the likelihood that the educational manager will render a superficial decision when he must respond quickly.

In other words, the educational manager who has adopted a theoretical approach to his work will seldom need to "shoot from the hip." When it is necessary, his aim is likely to be better.

Decision making is discussed in greater detail in Chapter 8, which relates it to theory and to contemporary scholarship and offers meaningful interpretations for the educational manager.

Theory Serves as a Guide to New Knowledge

Robert Townsend, writing in the best-seller, *Up the Organization,* said that "good organizations are living bodies that grow new muscles to meet challenges."[7] Similarly, the educational manager who has developed a style of operation based on the continuous and consistent use of a well-defined set of theory constructs should expect to gain new knowledge as he progresses. New ways to solve problems should result. It may be found that some courses of action (attempted solutions) prove to be more effective than others under similar sets of circumstances. The process by which problems are identified and analyzed, alternative courses of action formulated and considered—and tested—can become more conscious and more objective, leading to a better evaluation of the results obtained.

Projecting a course of action (forming a kind of operational hypothesis, or developing an "if-then" situation) is especially relevant to this point. Roaden expressed it well when he said:

> Theorizing involves utilizing what was (the past) for associating what is (the present) with what ought to be (the future). Stated another way, the purpose of theory is prediction-projection into the future. The accumulation of new knowledge can come about no other way.[8]

In summary, the use of theory in educational management enables the manager to evaluate continuously and to add to the known knowledge about organizational operation. New knowledge which may be gained from use of the theory process not only offers evidence regarding the success or failure of a given undertaking but also information upon which additional theoretical assumptions can be made—which can, in turn, be used to generate yet additional hypotheses to be tested.

Assaults Likely to be Made on the Manager's Theory Base

Once the educational manager successfully develops a conscious and consistent set of theoretical constructs to guide his operation, he may find the underpinning frequently under attack. Some of these attacks will come, quite properly, from within the manager himself as he constantly reexamines his attitudes, his values, and his outlook on education and on society. His theoretical and philosophical beliefs will naturally be tested within the context of these reexaminations; his views should not be regarded as being immutable. Actually, changes should come about as a result of the theory process described above. Indeed, one of the advantages cited was the likelihood that new information would be gained.

But it is the "staying hitched" aspect of this chapter that we are addressing here—resisting the temptation to change methods of operation for reasons which do not result from use of the theory process itself.

Let us look at several of the more frequently found pressures, threats, and assaults made on the educational manager's operational style.

Conflicting Expectations from Within and Without

One of the administrator's most difficult roles is facing expectations from many diverse publics,—expectations that often are in conflict with each other and, more seriously, in conflict with organizational policy and objectives. Although they relate it to a different point (the school as a social system), Roald F. Campbell and others illustrate this problem with the concept of the "administrator in the middle."

> Conflicts within some of the reference groups have been very well documented. Ordinarily, the people of a community are not of one mind. One public, for instance, may wish the school to provide a program of released time for religious education, while another public opposes any such idea. One public may advocate extensive provisions for vocational education, while another public would leave all such efforts to industry. One public may place great stress upon the intellectual purposes of the school, while another public would give almost equal emphasis to social purposes. These conflicts may become so sharp that they furnish the battleground for conflicts between competing leadership groups in the community.[9]

A real problem is how to deal effectively with numerous publics that have different and often conflicting expectations about what an organization's procedures or objectives should be. But our main concern here is the effect of those expectations on the administrator's established pattern of operation once it is "hitched" to a consciously developed theoretical base. A true case offers a good illustration. During the era when public schools were first required to move decisively toward the desegregation of their student bodies, a superintendent in a southern state rendered strong and courageous leadership to his board. He helped them recognize both the inevitability of desegregation and, to an extent, their moral obligation to do so. He helped develop a good understanding of the fact that blacks in that system had experienced inferior schools and were, under the new arrangement, in dire need of remedial and compensatory education. The superintendent was successful in securing federal funds for such programs, but only so long as the system maintained a visible and affirmative movement toward the development of a unitary system.

A sizable and vocal block of citizens objected to the speed with which the schools were moving toward a unitary system. They held a mass meeting at the courthouse, protested vigorously, and in the process demanded the dismissal of the superintendent who, in their opinion, was moving much faster than the law required and faster than neighboring school systems. The local board held firm and refused to initiate dismissal procedures. Within two weeks after the protest meeting, the superintendent was notified that federal funds for the compensatory program were being withheld, subject to a hearing, because insufficient progress was being made toward the development of a unitary school system.

This case turned out well. The superintendent held firmly to his beliefs, convinced Washington that significant desegregation was being achieved, and received strong backing from the board of education.

Similar conflicts can be easily imagined, or, in the case of practicing educational managers, recalled from experience. Students' expectations are often significantly different from those of their parents and of their teachers. It is not uncommon for local and state regulatory policies to conflict with those of accrediting agencies. And there is sometimes the local politician, the alumnus with a good record of financial donation, or the local patron with a friend in state government, who wants a special favor which requires extraordinary and potentially dangerous deviations from established policy or the manager's best judgment.

How is the educational manager to handle cases such as these? Some would suggest that he develop political and diplomatic skills, and such skills are certainly helpful. But in the long run he will be better served if he has formulated a deeply ingrained set of theoretical concepts, has acquired the ability to analyze and evaluate the pressures being applied in light of these concepts, and has the courage to act in terms of the course of action suggested by these beliefs. Tact, diplomacy, and good verbal skills will still serve him well, of course, but his best hope will lie in his ability to address these questions in perspective and to formulate solutions accordingly.

The Challenge of Change

It would be a mistake to conclude at this point that once the educational manager has developed his theoretically-based mode of operation that it will remain his loyal servant, with perhaps only minor adjustments needed from time to time. This is not true. The generation of new knowledge brings, in turn, new hypotheses to be tested. In this sense, the educational manager should welcome changes which relate closely to educational organizations, for they hold potential for bringing about improvements, both in terms of organizational achievements and his performance as well.

However, change often poses serious problems for the educational manager, especially if the change threatens the theoretical constructs which he has developed to guide his performance. Recognizing that many descriptive terms are being used today to describe changes (such as, change is occurring at exponential rates; all changes are not necessarily good; changes, per se, are neutral, we determine whether they become good or bad), it is sufficient here to refer only to the rapidity of change, and to the fact that some changes conflict with and tend to counteract others and some challenge his philosophical beliefs. This is yet another front on which the educational manager battles to maintain his theoretically based style of operation.

Consider the college administrator, for example, with program responsibilities. Having successfully led his staff through a substantial redesign of the curriculum, he is jarred from his satisfaction by several new developments which, at least on the surface, raise serious doubts about the efficacy of the new program. Does he hold fast to the newly developed program for fear that additional changes too soon would signal a hidden dissatisfaction with it? Or does he investigate the new developments openly, perhaps even with the hope that additional change would be welcome if it seemed to hold good promise for further improvements in the curriculum?

How the educational manager reacts to this kind of change will, again, be best answered by testing it against his theoretical moorings. How does he view program developments? How does program development occur most effectively? Who should be involved in program development? What evidence is required to warrant the adoption of new program components?

Numerous other changes could be illustrated. What are the implications of the new lifestyles of students on the policies governing behavior in high schools and colleges? How is the administrator to keep personnel practices attuned to changing legal opinions which are based on new court findings? What happens if court findings suggest the adoption of a policy and procedure which contradicts the manager's commitment to the worth and dignity of the individual (which could be a tenet of the theoretically-based operation he has developed)?

The point here is that the change process, though inevitable and often desirable, complicates the educational manager's style of operation, even though he may have developed this style extremely well and with a sound theoretical base. We believe that he can react to change more effectively when he has the benefit of a theoretically developed system of operation, but changes are certain to pose problems in maintaining it and keeping it viable.

The Constant Battle Between Leadership and Administration

Educational managers have often been fatal victims of the conflict between administration and leadership—a seemingly never-ending conflict. Unless his responsibilities are clearly defined in the areas of administration (defined here in terms of the mechanics of management) or leadership (defined here as that ability to assist individuals and groups to move toward mutually acceptable goals), the manager almost certainly runs the risk of being caught in this struggle. The manner in which he proposes to cope with this conflict should be part of whatever operational pattern he chooses to develop and follow. Achieving an effective balance between the administrative and leadership demands of his role is a constant challenge, especially as the age of accountability requires increased data gathering, more and longer reports to an ever increasing number of agencies, and other similar demands on the administrator's time and energy. Often these demands are necessary and legitimate, but time spent on them keeps him from people—including those involved in program development committees and students.

The educational manager who prides himself on keeping a clean and orderly desk, answering his mail promptly, and meeting all deadlines may, in the face of ever increasing demands for leadership (meeting with people, working on programs with faculty and students) find himself caught in a dilemma. A similar dilemma may face the educational manager who inclines toward the leadership role, places high priority on interacting with people (working with faculty, student and community groups) and attempts to influence and contribute to state and national movements, but is also responsible for the various and sundry mechanical duties associated with his assignment.

These and other similar problems relate to role definition, which depends largely on how the educational manager establishes priorities. They relate, also, to the question of what kind of managerial team can best serve the organization, what kind of person should do a specific job, and which of the various organizational tasks can and should be delegated. These are proper concerns of the eductional manager whose responsibility is to devise and manage some system for identifying, procuring, and coordinating the resources necessary to achieve designated organizational purposes. These matters are, therefore, additional examples of assaults made upon the manager's adopted style of operation—even if it is well-thought out and undergirded with time-tested theoretical constructs.

The Fraternal Nature of Education

It is likely that any effective operational pattern for the educational manager will include heavy emphasis on the worth and dignity of the individual and on consideration of others in the normal course of events within educational organizations. We argue for the inclusion of this component. At the same time, however, as we pointed out in Chapter 1, the concern for organizational productivity must be given high priority. Herein lies another possible dilemma for the educational manager, and another possible source of stress upon his operational methodology and philosophy.

For the purpose of illustration, let us assume that the theoretical plan guiding a particular educational manager does include concern both for the individual and for organizational productivity. Let us assume further that this hypothetical construct includes a provision for evaluation of performance and that an evaluation has revealed inadequate performance on the part of one person within the organization.

For example, the president of a medium-size college was unwilling to dismiss one of his vice presidents or move him to another position more compatible with his competency. The president's unwillingness stemmed from his personal concern for the welfare of the vice president. A concern for organizational goals (productivity) resulted in a decision to redefine the vice president's position in such a way as to exclude those responsibilities not being performed satisfactorily and transfer them to other vice presidents and deans who were performing well. Thus, one person's feelings and reputation were *protected* at the expense of overloading his associates—hardly an equitable solution.

The education profession tends to be highly protective of its members. This protection can result in pressure, applied or self-imposed, to overlook unsatisfactory performance and to make appropriate adjustments to accommodate it. As Lawrence J. Peter explained in his humorous yet helpful essay entitled *The Peter Principle,*[10] practices motivated by our concern for the individual often may harm him. Such concern is insufficient reason to promote a person who is performing satisfactorily to another position which exceeds his level of competence, thus sentencing him to be a victim of Peter's second principle, namely, "In a hierarchy, every employee tends to rise to his level of incompetence."

Summary

In this chapter we made a case for the contention that theory should be regarded as an essential ingredient in effective manager performance, rather than merely a topic for discussion by intellectually oriented professors and writers. Evidence was offered that, in fact, all educational managers operate consciously or unconsciously from a theoretical base. It was shown that artistic educational managers operate from a well-defined, thoughtfully-developed, and thoroughly-internalized philosophical and theoretical base. Finally we described a process by which this could be done.

Second, we suggested that several benefits accrue to the educational manager who views and uses theory in this way. Among these benefits were (1) lending purpose and direction to management, (2) providing justification and explanation of action taken, (3) promoting consistency in behavior, (4) resisting miscellaneous behavior, and (5) serving as a guide to new knowledge.

Finally, we raised several warning signals, alerting the educational manager to various kinds of assaults frequently made against his chosen operational style. We pointed out that the educational manager finds himself caught up in the constant fight between administration and leadership, between a concern for the individual and for organizational goals (productivity), between diverse and often conflicting expectations from the various publics whom he is expected to serve, and between changes which point toward progress and those which push the organization backward.

DISCUSSION QUESTIONS/LEARNING ACTIVITIES

1. What are the major tenets of the operational theory which guides your day-to-day activities as an educational manager? If you are not presently engaged in educational management, identify a person who is, and who is well-known to you, and identify major operational principles that seem to undergird his performance.

2. Have you ever worked with an educational manager who was caught in what we describe as the constant battle between administration and leadership? If so, what was the outcome? What effect did the outcome have on the educational manager's performance? On the organization?

3. To what extent do you think that educational managers are inclined to attract staff members who share their theoretical/philo-

sophical principles? Assuming that managers are so inclined, what do you think would be the long-range impact of such a practice on organizational climate?

4. In the sciences, theory is generally perceived to have three major purposes—to explain, to predict, to control. Are these three purposes applicable to theory in educational management? Give examples to illustrate your point-of-view.

5. What is a principle worth? Interview an educational manager who was released from his position because of his stand on a point of principle. Relate his retrospective evaluation of his action to the points made by the authors in this section.

6. Arrange for an interview with a practicing educational manager who can describe a situation in which he "stayed hitched" on a point of principle. What principle was involved? What were the antecedents and consequences of his "staying hitched?"

NOTES

1. Warren Barr Knox, *Eye of the Hurricane* (Corvallis: Oregon State University Press, 1973), p. 82.

2. E. Grady Bogue, "An Inquiry Into the Nature of Scientific Theory and Its Relationship to Educational Administration," *Educational Quest,* College of Education, Memphis State University, Vol. XV, No. 1, Winter (1971), p. 26.

3. Orin B. Graff, Calvin M. Street, Ralph B. Kimbrough and Archie R. Dykes, *Philosophical Theory and Practice in Educational Administration* (Belmont, Calif.: Wadsworth, 1966), p. 12.

4. Robert L. Saunders, Ray C. Phillips, and Harold T. Johnson, *A Theory of Educational Leadership* (Columbus: Charles E. Merrill, 1966), p. 5.

5. Ibid., pp. 6-10.

6. Arliss L. Roaden, "An Analysis and Synthesis of Theory Constructs in Educational Administration" (Ph.D. dissertation, University of Tennessee, Knoxville, 1961), p. 34.

7. Robert Townsend, *Up the Organization* (New York: Alfred A. Knopf, 1970), p. 134.

8. Roaden, "Theory Constructs," p. 202.

9. Roald F. Campbell, Edwin M. Bridges, John E. Corbally, Jr., Raphael O. Nystrand, and John A. Ramseyer, *Introduction to Educational Administration,* 4th edition (Boston: Allyn and Bacon, 1971), p. 260.

10. Laurence J. Peter, *The Peter Principle* (New York: William Morrow, 1969), p. 7.

5
Organizing as a Management Art

*The organizational geography of super-industrial
society can be expected to become increasingly
kinetic, filled with turbulence and change. The
more rapidly the environment changes, the shorter
the life span of organizational forms. In administrative
structure, just as in architectural structure, we are
moving from long-enduring to temporary forms,
from permanence to transience. We are moving
from bureaucracy to ad-hocracy.*

Alvin Toffler, *Future Shock*

During the last few years, the authors became familiar with
two large universities that were similar in institutional role,
enrollment size and mix, academic program structure, and
community environment. A specific set of operating factors
was available on one of the administrative activities in these
institutions—admissions and registration. The difference in
the admissions-registrar operating budgets for the two
schools was large. In one school, the total clerical and professional staff numbered approximately 35; and the annual
operating budget was approximately $350,000. In the other,
the staff numbered 120 and the annual budget was close to
$1,100,000!

Comparisons of this sort are hazardous indeed. But even
when allowances are made for differences in the cost of operation and differences in functional activities, there remains a
serious question as to why the budgetary patterns of the two
offices were so different. In the office with the larger budget
it was evident that there was an excessive fragmentation of
job specialities—a clerk for the "A" records, a clerk for the

This chapter was adapted from a paper originally appearing in the October 1971
issue of *Phi Delta Kappan*, pp. 94-96. Used by permission.

"B" records, and a supervisor for every two clerks. There were no less than four layers of supervision between the base position in the office and the director of the activity. Cells comprised of two or three clerks and a supervisor were isolated throughout the office and had little communication or contact with other organizational units. The telephone lines were the only common element, and these were so confused and complex that they did not provide any real service to the students.

Upon arriving on the job, a newly appointed admissions officer-registrar observed that his most pressing problem was finding enough toilet facilities for 120 people. Placing personal service to students high on his priorities and using a keen sense of organizational artistry, this academic administrator within a year reduced the size of the staff from over 120 to less than 80 and cut the operating budget by more than a quarter of a million dollars.

The task required courage as well as organizational artistry. His reorganization of the office and deletion of some positions pitted him against the state civil service system and generated reverberations throughout the institution. When one stops to consider that a quarter of a million dollars is enough to operate a modest size academic department for a year, this investment of managerial knowledge and courage commands additional appreciation.

Knowledge of organizational concepts can produce educational environments which are more effective and efficient. How many dollars flow into unproductive administrative activities each year in our schools and colleges—dollars that should be going to program activities—because the educational manager responsible for the activity lacks organizational artistry? The answer would be interesting and perhaps alarming.

The ability to conceive and breathe life into new organizational structures may well be one of the most critical competencies needed by educational management in the 70s. The character of these structures is a key variable in determining (1) how well we accomplish our educational goals, (2) what degree of fulfillment persons within the structure obtain, and (3) what efficiency is realized in terms of resource utilization.

Many administrators are well versed in the classical concepts of organization—"span of control," "division of labor," and "chain of command." Yet the evidence from both theorists and practitioners is that traditional organizational fabrics show severe signs of strain under the pressures of a fast-changing society. Are there organizational patterns which can revitalize our educational organizations so that they will become more responsive, more flexible, and more exciting places? Disposable (temporary or task force) organizations offer possibilities for the renewal that is necessary for the performance of contemporary educational tasks. In developing this theme, we will briefly review some of the dysfunctions of traditional organizational patterns and then consider the merits of disposable patterns.

Dysfunctions of Traditional Structures

The concept of an organization as a static series of line and staff relationships does not account for the impact of informal structures. The study of group dynamics reveals that every individual in an organization is a member of both informal and formal groups and that these groups can have an impact—constructive and destructive—on attitudes and behavior.

A second limitation of traditional organizational patterns is that they do not encourage a "systems" view of the environment. Organizations do not exist in a social and economic vacuum, but are parts of large systems. Administrators must be attuned to the dynamic transactions of organizations with their external environment.

One of the most critical indictments is that these patterns reduce the opportunity for individuals to achieve self-actualization. The principles of scientific management—which include the familiar ideas of chain of command, span of control, task specialization, etc.—combine restrictive managerial controls with jobs fragmented by technology and specialization. Another serious criticism of contemporary organizational structures is that they contribute to inertia by reducing opportunity for change. In the words of Victor Thompson, "A hierarchical system always favors the status quo."[1]

Thompson also suggests that in modern organizations there is a growing imbalance between ability and authority—between the right to make decisions, which is authority, and the power to do so, which is specialized ability. Although today's society is one of specialization and increased inter-dependence, we find it difficult to integrate specialists into hierarchical organizational patterns.

Finally, contemporary organizational patterns may encourage a mechanistic view of organizational functions—a failure to recognize that the vitality of an organization depends upon the vitality of each component.

What kinds of organizational patterns can loosen up the rigidities of traditional structure, provide the quick response needed for problem-solving, and nurture the talents and energies of an increasing array of specialists? Some organizations have sought solutions in the processes of decentralization. The creation of semiautonomous units does bring decision making closer to the point where problems occur. Decentralization is a popular move because people want to be involved. However involvement is not the only variable of importance in the decision to decentralize an organization.

Though we may cut our organizational pie into smaller sectors, the rigidities associated with the larger unit may follow us into the smaller ones, unless we find new structural strategies. Chris Argyris has suggested that organizational structures will be adapted to the type of decision problem engaged:

> . . . organizations (of the future) will tend to vary the structures they use according to the kinds of decision that must be made. If one asks the individual in the organization of the future to see the company organization chart, he will be asked, "For what type of decision?"[2]

Argyris outlines four types of structures and matches them with the character of decision problems. He suggests that the structure of involvement will be conditioned by the complexity of the decision, the breadth and time of decision impact, and the resources available to make the decision.

Concept of a Disposable Organization

"Throw-away" organization patterns, or disposable organizations, are tools of prime interest. The emergence of such organizational patterns is discussed by Alvin Toffler in *Future Shock*.

> The high rate of turnover (in organizational relationships) is most dramatically symbolized by the rapid rise of what executives call "project" or "task force" management. Here teams are assembled to solve specific short-term problems. Then, exactly like mobile playgrounds, they are disassembled and their human components reassigned. Sometimes teams are thrown together to serve only for a few days. Sometimes they are intended to last a few years. But unlike the functional departments or divisions of a traditional bureaucratic organization, which are presumed to be permanent, the project or task force team is temporary by design.[3]

The flowering of organizations with self-destruct mechanisms would appear to be a common occurrence in our fast-paced and rapidly changing society. The birth of institutes and centers in higher education, as described by Paul L. Dressel and others in *The Confidence Crisis,*[4] and more recently by Stanley O. Ikenberry and Renee C. Friedman in *Beyond Academic Departments,*[5] is one manifestation of special structures that are born out of the failure of traditional structures to react to change. Certainly there is nothing radically new in the idea of specially designed structures to meet special needs. What is new is the frequency with which such structures have come into operation over the past few years.

William H. Read,[6] Warren Bennis,[7] and Ronald J. Ross[8] have described the application of these concepts in the business and industrial world. Disposable organizations also offer promise of being an effective antidote to the "bureaupathology" that causes relationships in contemporary educational structures to fossilize. Task force structures summoned into action to deal with issue-oriented tasks can provide both flexibility and adaptability. Such temporary structures can furnish challenges essential to the renewal of both organizations and persons within them. Other advantages these structures provide are the opportunity to harmonize an array of specialists in a common venture and focus on problem-oriented tasks, which diminishes concern for the status of position and gives more weight to the authority of competence.

We would be naive to believe that these structures would not be afflicted with the same ills associated with bureaucracy. Important in the concept of the disposable organization is the knowledge that these structures are temporary in nature. There should be clear recognition of and provision for a "self-destruct" process when the problem or issue is resolved.

Though Toffler praises the contribution of the ad-hoc organization, our conviction is that most persons will need a degree of stability along with the challenge of change. We should be able to capture the best of both by providing the basic stability and security that is necessary for persons to enjoy the challenge of risk when they participate in the temporary tensions of the disposable organization.

To summarize, the essential characteristics of disposable organizations are:

1. They are *problem-* or *issue-centered* rather than functionally centered.

2. They are *temporary* structures. There is a built-in "self-destruct" process which is activated upon problem resolution.

3. They will be staffed so that the *authority of competence* replaces the authority of position and role.

4. They will offer *"short circuit" channels of communication* rather than the carefully contained vertical patterns of hierarchy.

The Application of Disposable Organizations

What are some of the practical ways in which such arrangements might serve the interest of our educational organizations? Let us examine a hypothetical case, that of the newly appointed Dean of a College of Education for a large university. His college is organized into the following departments:

Educational Administration
Secondary Education

Elementary Education
Guidance and Personnel Services
Health and Physical Education
Special Education

Among the organizational problems confronting him are:

1. The college is structured in a mixed fashion. Some departments are organized on a functional basis (i.e., administration is a functional activity reaching across all levels of education) while others are organized on an applied basis (for example, is secondary education a content area or a level where knowledge is applied?).

2. The department of elementary education is extremely broad in span of control. The chairman must cover the activities of over 30 faculty members with activities in methodology, learning foundations, and research.

3. The allegiance of some faculty members is mixed; some have principal concern for their content area (such as educational philosophy) while others have a particular fondness for the problems of certain educational levels (higher education, for example).

How might he apply the principle of disposable organizations in providing a more vital and productive framework? One possibility would be a "matrix" type of structure in which one dimension would revolve around instructional content or areas of knowledge—a dimension that would also roughly define the graduates of the college (such as teachers, administrators, and counselors). The other dimension of our matrix would be the temporary or "disposable" element—which would serve as the vehicle for the research and service concern of the college. Figure 5 illustrates these structures.

The disciplinary departments would furnish a basic "organizational home" for all members of the faculty. These principal structures would provide security and stability. In the disposable structures, members of the faculty with special interests, talents, and experience at the different levels of

Figure 5

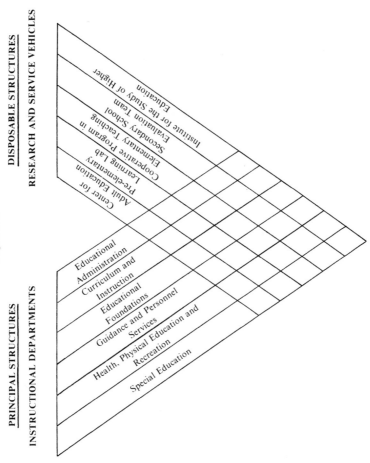

education would focus their energy on the research and service needs of the college. Thus, selected members of the faculty could form:

1. a center for adult education,
2. a pre-elementary learning laboratory,
3. a cooperative program in elementary teaching,
4. a secondary school evaluation team,
5. an institute for the study of higher education.

These temporary structures would result from such factors as community need, faculty interest and talent, and adequate resources. The dissipation of the need or withdrawal of resources does not threaten the faculty since its basic security would be provided in the disciplinary organization.

This matrix structure can provide an interesting marriage of traditional and disposable elements. It might also generate a productive tension between the world of research and the world of reality. The actual application of the concept, however, may not be without practical limitations.

For example, the existence of "two bosses" for each member of the faculty—one in instruction and the other in research and service—may prove troublesome to both faculty and administration. The success of any structure depends in large measure upon the commitment of those in that structure. Thus, our concept may look enticing on paper and fail miserably in practice. Similarly, there are some structural arrangements which defy translation to organizational charts, but which in fact work very well. At least the concept may prove of stimulus value as we reflect on the practical problems of organization.

Summary

Disposable organizations can be used as tools for organizational renewal and are problem-centered rather than function-centered structures. They are temporary structures summoned into action to deal with particular needs and disassembled when the need is met. Staff relationships within disposable organizations rely on the authority of competence rather than on the authority of position or role. Patterns of communication follow a "critical path" toward task fulfillment rather than moving up and down hierarchial channels.

The educational administrator should not attempt to resolve structural problems without full consideration of the other variables which can confound the best laid organizational plans. If we have learned anything about educational management over the past few years, it is that the task of management is one compounded of both science and art. From the scientific study of organizations we have learned of the interacting impact of structure, group membership, individual personality, and managerial philosophy. The artistry of management begins with a sure knowledge of these variables and culminates in their orchestration.

An example of this point of interaction among management concepts is found in the work of the admissions officer-registrar discussed at the beginning of this chapter. He did not entirely accomplish his reorganization via the simple expediency of revising structural arrangements and enlarging job responsibilities. He also brought technology to focus on the problems he faced by having a complete reexamination of the communication patterns within the office, especially the telephone system. With the assistance of professionals in this area, he was able to install a new, more effective phone system that was a significant aid in improving the revised organizational structure. He also nurtured informal relationships among staff members by enlarging and redecorating the lounge space—space made available by reducing the size of the original staff.

Thus, the educational manager operates in a socio-technical framework. Organizational structures are important tools that he can apply artistically in creating a more effective educational environment.

DISCUSSION QUESTIONS/LEARNING ACTIVITIES

1. To what extent is the organizational form of an institution a reflection of the personalities and talent in the institution? How do you evaluate this interaction of organizational and personality?

2. Many educational organizations are characterized as "bureau-cracies." Review the original work of Max Weber on bureaucracy and the work of more recent organizational scholars. What are the characteristics of a bureacracy? Are these necessarily negative? What gives the word "bureaucracy" its negative connotation?

3. The organizational scholar Victor Thompson, cited in this chapter, has used the term "bureaupathology." What is meant by this term?

4. How would you evaluate a proposed organizational arrange-ment against a current arrangement? What factors and criteria might be used?

5. Prepare an analytical report on the organization for education at the state level in your state. How did the current organization emerge? How are higher education, technical education, elemen-tary-secondary education related? What recent changes have oc-curred and what changes are imminent?

6. Utilize the concept of "adhocracy" or "disposable" organiza-tional structures in a staff study to illustrate how an educational institution known to you might function more effectively with appli-cation of the concept.

NOTES

1. Victor Thompson, *Modern Organizations* (New York: Alfred Knopf, 1961), p. 61.
2. Chris Argyris, *Integrating the Individual and the Organization* (New York: John Wiley and Sons, 1964), pp. 211-12.
3. Alvin Toffler, *Future Shock* (New York: Random House, 1970), p. 119.
4. Paul L. Dressel et al., *The Confidence Crisis* (San Francisco: Jos-sey Bass, 1970).
5. Stanley O. Ikenberry and Renee C. Friedman, *Beyond Academic Departments* (San Francisco: Jossey Bass, 1972).
6. William H. Read, "The Decline of the Hierarchy in Industrial Organizations," *Business Horizons,* Fall 1965, pp. 71-75.
7. Warren Bennis, "Beyond Bureaucracy," *Trans-Action,* July-August 1965, pp. 31-35.
8. Ronald J. Ross, "Rotating Planners and Doers," *Harvard Busi-ness Review,* January-February 1962, pp. 101-115.

6
Using Authority Effectively

But man, proud man,
  Dressed in a little authority,
Most ignorant of what he's most assured,
  His glassy essence, like an angry ape,
Plays such fantastic tricks before high heaven
  As make the angels weep.

Shakespeare, *Measure for Measure*

In Scene Eleven of the play *Galileo* by Brecht, there is a symbolic display of the relationship between position and authority. At the opening of the scene, former Cardinal Barberini, now Pope Urban VII, stands clad only in his underclothes. As the Inquisitor stands nearby, Barberini reflects informally—almost affectionally— on Galileo the man and pays him tribute as the greatest physicist of the day. As he adds the vestments and finally the papal crown, however, Barberini's observations change in tone and content, reflecting more clearly the authority invested in Pope Urban VIII. He consents to the inquisition of Galileo, insisting only that the inquisition not include torture.[1]

We are inclined to observe that this is a shallow covering for the exercise of such authority and feel that such an attitude could only exist in the Middle Ages. But this is not the case. Too many educational managers continue to play the part of Barberini today. Authority is a concept often misunderstood and misused by educational managers. Yet the artistic use of authority can increase one's effectiveness. For this reason, it may be useful for the educational manager to review his understanding of the concept.

Traditionally, educational communities have preferred not to think in terms of power and authority relationships. This reluctance is easily understood because educational communities have placed high value on reason, consensus, and involvement.

The uneasy feelings concerning authority are thoughtfully explored by Llewellyn Gross who points out that

> . . .authority rests in part upon criteria which perpetuate inequalities in sex, class, ethnic membership, and nepotism and economic inheritance.[2]

He suggests further that hierarchal authority is perpetuated through a variety of status devices that are inappropriate for an environment that values knowledge, skill, and merit.

Moreover, Gross raises questions about the status of administrative skill and concomitant authority in the following passage:

> It is said that organizational coordination is a competence or skill available only to administrative experts. But is this skill really much different from the clerical and interpersonal competence of many white collar employees with college level education?[3]

In one of the more provocative papers on higher education administration to appear in recent years, the precarious nature of the authority of educational managers at that level is traced by Terry Lunsford.

> . . .the special competence of the academic administrator is highly precarious and contingent. In the first place, there is no esoteric specialty of "higher education" as an entity that academic men generally will acknowledge today and in which university administrators might claim a trained and systematic "competence" akin to that of an academic discipline. Second, no expertise in governance (or administration, or management) is accepted by most academic men as a specialty that might undergird the special functions that administrators have come to perform. Thus, university specialists in administration today cannot convincingly claim, as a group, any distinctive experience which might clothe their bare, formal positions with "professional" legitimacy. In the highly professional organization that is a university, this alone means that their very authority is always more or less precarious.[4]

Though we admire the scholarship of these writers, we do not agree with the notion that being a white-collar college graduate ipso facto endows one with the kind of management competence needed in schools and colleges today. Nor do we hold the opinion that authority is not a viable concept for educational organizations.

Indeed, the need for authority is just as keen in educational organizations as in any other kind of organization. The problem is that too many educational managers misuse authority. As Samuel Johnson pointed out years ago, "lawful and settled authority is very seldom resisted when it is well employed." In our mind, therefore, the question before educational managers and educational organizations is not whether authority is appropriate but how it should be artistically applied. Yves Simon has captured the essential issue forcefully:

> However vague and ill-defined our concepts of authority and liberty may be, we realize at once that authority and liberty are at the same time antinomic and complementary. . . As to their complementary character, it is quite clear that authority, when it is not fairly balanced by liberty is but tyranny, and that liberty, when it is not fairly balanced by authority, is but abusive licence. . .There would be hardly any exaggeration in the statement that the essential question for every social group is that of combining rightly the forces of authority and liberty.[5]

Our theme is that the educational manager has available the same patterns of authority that are available to managers in any type of organized enterprise. The question is not whether authority is appropriate for the educational manager but how he might best exercise it. To deal with this challenge, we will briefly explore the nature and functions of authority and the kinds of authority that the educational manager can exercise, and then treat the matter of applying them.

Nature and Function of Authority

Yves Simon has defined authority as "an active power, residing in a person and exercised through a command, that is through a practical judgment to be taken as a rule of conduct by the free will of another person."[6] He goes further to identify the essential function of authority: "to assure the unity of action of a united multitude. A multitude aiming at a common good which can be attained only through a common action must be united in its action by some steady principle. This principle is precisely what we call authority."[7]

Herbert Simon has defined authority as "the power to make decisions which guide the actions of another."[8] He suggests three basic functions of authority. The first of these is to force the conformity of the individual to norms laid down by the group or organization. A second function is to secure the contribution of expertise in decision making. The third is to secure coordination of individuals and groups. The difference between the second and third functions is that the second promotes a "good" decision and the third focuses groups on enactment of the decision.

Chester Barnard indicates that "authority is the character of a communication (order) in a formal organization by virtue of which it is accepted by a contributor or member of the organization as governing or determining what he does or is not to do so far as the organization is concerned."[9] Barnard lists four conditions needed for the proper application of authority and its acceptance:

> A person can and will accept a communication as authoritative only when four conditions simultaneously obtain: (1) he can and does understand the communication; (2) *at the time of his decision*, he believes that it is not inconsistent with the purpose of the organization; (3) *at the time of his decision*, he believes it to be compatible with his personal interests as a whole; and (4) he is able mentally and physically to comply with it.[10]

Thus, Barnard emphasizes the "acceptance" theory of authority. This theory was expounded in Machiavelli's *The Prince*, in which the author pointed out that the continued existence of all government depended on the consent of the masses. Contrary to the traditional manner of viewing authority, the acceptance theory indicates that authority flows from the bottom to the top rather than from the top to the bottom.

Barnard helps us understand this idea better by means of the following quote taken from Major General James G. Harbord's *The American Army in France*:

> . . .the greatest of all democracies is an army. Discipline and morale influence the inarticulate vote that is taken internally by masses of men when the order comes to move forward—a variant of the crowd psychology that inclines it to follow a leader, but the army does not move forward until the motion has "carried." "Unanimous consent" only follows cooperation between the individual men in the ranks.[11]

This illustration serves as an important reminder to those who hold management responsibility, that even when the regimen is a rigorous one and even when physical force may be involved, authority still rests on the consent of individuals.

Patterns of Authority

The German sociologist Max Weber first characterized modes of authority as rational-legal, functional, traditional, and charismatic. Rational-legal authority is based on the assumption that an organization seeks the good of everyone and thus merits support. Traditional authority is based on the belief that an organization and its norms for behavior are hallowed by age and experience and should not be challenged. Charismatic authority rests on faith and confidence in the values and goals of organizational leaders. The framework we propose for viewing patterns of authority is somewhat similar to Weber's and was suggested by William J. Onchen.[12]

The Authority of Competence

Most importantly, the educational manager has available to him the authority of managerial competence. Kenneth Benne has called this the "authority of the expert." He indicated that "expert authority, like all authority, stems from the dependence of human beings, with many and diverse needs, upon the assistance of other persons and groups possessed with greater resources for meeting those needs."[13] Performance—not pedigree—marks the pathway to the authority of competence. We earn the allegiance of those with whom we work only if they come to trust the specialized knowledge and skill that we manifest as effective educational managers.

In summary, the educational manager's claim to authority ideally finds its root in his managerial competence and in the technical training and skill needed to effectively integrate policy, personnel, and programs.

The Authority of Personality

Some educational managers have good ideas that are born out of intelligence and energy. But sometimes these ideas never receive the attention they deserve because of the obnoxious personalities of their proponents. A systems analyst whose brilliance in bringing order out of chaos in information flow may be unexcelled, but his authority of competence will never be fully utilized unless he develops an ability to create productive working relationships with other people. This does not mean that a manager needs to smile all the time. Such falseness would be worse than honest irritability. What it does mean, however, is that we must cultivate personalities which enable us to work in reasonable harmony with other persons.

The Authority of Character

William J. Onchen suggests that the authority of character is in essence:

> ...your "credit rating" with other people as to your integrity, reliability, honesty, loyalty, sincerity, personal morals, and ethics.[14]

One may think that this sounds more like a description of a good Boy Scout. But to those professionals who have stepped outside the moral boundaries that society considers acceptable, these words are more than rhetoric. If a person's behavior tramples on the dignity of another person, he will not be trusted very far. If he rips the fabric of someone's personal integrity, then he diminishes his opportunity to take full advantage of whatever authority of competence he possesses.

The Authority of Position

The authority of position enables a manager to force compliance because of sanctions, financial or other, associated with the position. This kind of authority is often minimized in the managerial literature—and especially in schools and colleges—because it suggests the exercise of raw power. Such exercise may bring temporary compliance but long term animosity.

Educational managers are required to be masters of persuasive relationships. But there are times when the exercise of the authority of position is not only appropriate but essential. The school principal who decides that he cannot support his superintendent and school board in their goal for greater racial equality may find his superintendent's clarification of "options" (get behind the policy or get out) stressful but certainly not inappropriate. The college dean who requires that one of his department chairmen repay the university a thousand dollars because the latter took several of his faculty on a 1500-mile retreat to Las Vegas may be characterized as an authoritarian—but he is also right.

The Application of Authority

Cultivating the kinds of authority we have mentioned is a sizeable challenge in itself. But the real artistry comes in putting authority to work. When, for example, should one lead with the authority of personality and when with the authority of position? Several general rules can be suggested.

First, there is no principle of managerial conduct better established than one to the effect that orders will not be given that cannot or will not be obeyed. The educational manager must be careful in his use of authority so that he does not place himself in a "zero sum" situation in which if someone else wins, he loses. The artistic application of authority calls for one to lead with the authority that is most likely to produce acceptance. Leading with the authority of position, the principal of a school may order the custodian to tidy up the hallway. But he probably should use another approach when he wants a member of his faculty to do something.

Second, the artistic application of authority requires flexibility. In a meeting of a council of academic deans, there was a fascinating but ineffective display of authority. One council member took over two hours to explain in tedious detail the philosophical and technical bases for a new academic policy. What he failed to sense was that his colleagues were perfectly willing to accept his recommendation on the basis of his authority of competence. He insisted on an "overkill" exposition of the matter, thus alienating council members and unwittingly defeating a good idea.

Third, a manager should think carefully before he tries to use one kind of authority as a substitute for another. Suppose that you are a Dean of Admissions and Records in a university. The Director of Admissions comes in one morning and suggests a change in the admissions policy. The new policy, he explains, requires the use of a minimax strategy with multiple cutoffs in combination with a triple somersault discriminant analysis. Unwilling to admit that you do not have any notion of what the director is talking about, you nevertheless give a knowledgeable smile and—leading from the authority of personality—compliment him and say that this is exactly what you had in mind. Or you may turn down the idea because you cannot understand it, thus using the authority of position ineffectively. Either way, you lose the respect of the director because he knows that you do not really understand the idea. What you can do is exhibit both the authority of character and of competence by admitting that you do not understand the technical complexities but would be glad to listen to an explanation about the impact of the policy on the university and its students.

People have a way of cutting through any veneer that others use to cover up weaknesses. A person may be pleasant and possess character and a charming personality; but if he doesn't know anything, he will find his authority "bank account" overdrawn very quickly.

Finally, a manager's authority style influences both the behavior and development of those who hold management responsibility below his level. If he swings the weight of his authority, then subordinates will run scared. If he tightens control, then so will managers at lower levels. Authority applied without sensitivity and responsibility rests oppressively on the developmental potential of subordinates. And, it can deprive senior educational managers of the leadership initiative and creativity of middle-level managers, whose effective performance is the key to organization effectiveness and efficiency.

In a fascinating but disturbing report, psychologist Stanley Milgram reports an experiment in which one subject (the "teacher") was asked to administer electric shock to another subject (the "learner"). For the subject assuming the role of the teacher, the apparent purpose of the experiment was to explore the effect of punishment on learning. The subject playing the part of the learner was actually a confederate of the experimenter and received no shock but acted out his part as the "teacher" administered shocks ranging from 15 to 450 volts. The real purpose of the investigation was to see how far the "teacher" subjects would go in yielding to the authority of the experimenter.

The disquieting finding was that every subject participating in the experiment delivered at least one shock to the "learner" subject, and many were willing to administer very high voltages. Milgram's conclusion that ". . . even when the destructive effect of their work becomes painfully clear, and they are asked to carry out actions incompatible with fundamental standards of morality, relatively few people have the resources needed to resist authority . . . . Ordinary people, simply doing their jobs, and without any particular hostility on their part can become agents in a terrible destructive process."[15]

Results of this and similar studies that were taken against the backdrop of Nazi behavior in World War II are sufficient to make the educational manager approach his use of authority with increased responsibility and sensitivity.

Summary

We have suggested that an educational manager can improve the impact of his leadership by understanding and cultivating four kinds of authority.

1. *The authority of competence commands confidence.* It is composed of those knowledges and skills associated with the management function.
2. *The authority of personality commands rapport.* It is composed of those interpersonal abilities which enable one to relate positively and productively with staff and other colleagues.
3. *The authority of character commands respect.* It is composed of those marks of behavior which reveal one as a person of both professional and personal integrity.
4. *The authority of position commands obedience.* It is composed of those rights and sanctions associated with one's administrative position.

To understand and cultivate these modes of authority is only the first step in achieving more effective leadership performance. The artistic application of authority requires both flexibility and sensitivity, to ensure that one will lead with the mode of authority that promises to be most effective.

DISCUSSION QUESTIONS/LEARNING ACTIVITIES

1. What constructive function does authority serve in the life of organizations? Is there less need for the expression of authority in educational organizations than in business organizations?

2. To what extent is manager style and identity related to exercise of authority? That is, are educational managers who are insecure more likely to have authoritarian styles?

3. Can you think of a recent policy or program decision that was accepted or defeated not on the substance of the idea but on the personality of the person presenting or championing the idea?

4. Read the original work on authority by Max Weber, relevant passages from other writers such as Machiavelli and more recent commentators. Develop a paper that outlines your understanding of the nature and function of authority.

5. Using the report of Milgram's experiment cited in this chapter as a beginning, review the literature for other research work on the concept of authority. Develop a paper that summarizes what you found and its implications for administration.

6. Develop a decision diary for an educational manager you know. Identify those situations in which he or she led with the kinds of authority we've mentioned in this chapter. Analyze the decision type and setting associated with the expression of each kind of authority.

NOTES

1. Bertolt Brecht, *Galileo,* in *Modern Repretoire—Series Two,* Eric Bentley (ed.), (Denver: University of Denver Press, 1952). pp. 425-476.

2. Llewellyn Gross, "Hierarchical Authority in Educational Institutions," in *Administering Human Resources,* Frances M. Trusty (ed.), (Berkeley: McCutchan Publishing Corporation, 1971), p. 182.

3. *Ibid.,* p. 181.

4. Terry Lunsford, "Authority and Ideology in the Administered University," *The American Behavioral Scientist,* May-June 1968, p. 6.

5. Yves R. Simon, *Nature and Functions of Authority* (Milwaukee: Marquette University Press, 1948), pp. 1-2.

6. *Ibid.,* p. 6.

7. *Ibid.,* p. 17.

8. Herbert A. Simon, *Administrative Behavior: A Study of Decision-Making Processes in Administration Organization* (New York: The Free Press, 1967), p. 125.

9. Chester Barnard, *The Functions of the Executive* (Cambridge: Harvard University Press, 1966), p. 163.

10. *Ibid.,* p. 165.

11. James G. Harbord, *The American Army in France* (Boston: Little Brown and Co., 1936), p. 259.

12. For the concept of the four types of authority we are indebted to a paper entitled "The Authority to Manage," by William Onchen, Jr., published by the Industrial Relations Center, California Institute of Technology, Pasadena, California (1970).

13. Kenneth D. Benne, *A Conception of Authority* (New York: Teachers College, Columbia University, 1943).

14. Onchen, *"The Authority to Manage,"* p. 2.

15. Stanley Milgram, "The Dilemma of Obedience," *Phi Delta Kappan,* May 1974, p. 605.

7

The Influence of Manager Integrity and Identity

Insist on yourself; never imitate. Your own gift you can present every moment with the cumulative force of a whole life's cultivation; but of the adopted talent of another you have only an extemporaneous half possession. That which each can do best, none but his Maker can teach him.

Ralph Waldo Emerson, *Self Reliance*

Once a colleague shared with us some personal grievances which had been building to the point where the seeds of dissatisfaction would no longer lie dormant. The nature of his dissatisfaction, stimulated by the recent behavior of his new supervisor, was related more to the context of his position than to the content. After he had revealed the nature of his dissatisfaction, we asked whether he had shared his grievances with the supervisor. He replied that he had not because of his apprehension concerning the supervisor's reaction and the possible outcome of a "confrontation." We then posed the following questions:

1. How can your supervisor learn of your dissatisfaction? If you were in his place, would you like to learn of dissatisfaction via the organizational grapevine, or would you prefer colleagues with enough courage to speak directly?

2. Is it possible that there are conditions motivating your supervisor's behavior that you are not aware of?

3. Is it possible that this small conflict may produce a more viable relationship between you and your supervisor?

This chapter was adapted from a paper originally appearing in the April 1972 issue of *Phi Delta Kappan*, pp. 506-508. Used by permission.

4. Can such conflict have a positive effect on your administrative competence as well as that of your supervisor?

5. Do you prefer to get your dissatisfaction "out in the open" or keep it repressed and risk the probability that it will force its way out later in an inopportune way?

6. You assume that your supervisor may not receive your grievance in a supportive and open manner. In any case, shouldn't you find out immediately the stature of the man with whom you will be working?

We took these questions as a basis for an extended exploration of the relationship between managerial integrity and organizational health. On the next day, our colleague had the courage to share his point of view with his supervisor. To his pleasure, he discovered that he was working with a man who demonstrated a high degree of personal integrity and managerial maturity.

This illustration introduces an administrative attitude which is of paramount importance in the health and productivity of educational organizations. We will explore the relationship between managerial integrity and a productive organizational climate. What we shall say comes from both reflection and action. The authors of *Philosophic Theory and Practice in Educational Administration* suggest that:

> Perhaps the greatest need today in the ideological field is a willingness to test our ideas, to measure consequences one against the other as each is implemented . . . The highest form of objectivity and intellectual honesty is exercised when a person examines his basic philosophical concepts in terms of experience and displays his conclusions for public inspection. This involves the personal process of saying: I subscribe to these ideas. I have acted in this way with these results.[1]

In this chapter, our theme is that productivity increases when the educational manager acts to create a climate of honesty and trust. Though our premise is simply stated, the consequences of action are not so simple. To accept this proposition, educational managers must be willing to sustain threat to their self-esteem. They must also live with, and encourage, a degree of organizational tension and conflict. Thus, managerial integrity is a keystone in the arch of organizational health and productivity.

The Relationship of Managerial Integrity to Organizational Productivity

Some contemporary organizational theorists—such as Rensis Likert,[2] Chris Argyris,[3] Douglas McGregor[4]—have suggested that an organizational climate characterized by high trust stimulates high performance. Although there is not always a direct relationship between job satisfaction and job performance, greater productivity usually results when an organizational climate of dependence, submissiveness, conformity, and imposed evaluation gives way to relationships which foster trust, independence of action, risk taking, and self-evaluation. But how does the educational manager develop such an organizational climate? One way is through open communication where ideas are free to flow in all directions in the organizational hierarchy. William V. Haney describes a high-trust climate this way.

> The trust-performance cycles suggest an interesting parallel—the mutual dependency of a trusting relationship and effective communication performance. When the organizational climate can be characterized as trusting and supportive, communication practice is generally good. There are a number of reasons for this.
>
> First of all the members of such an organization, relatively speaking, have no ax to grind, nothing to be gained by miscommunicating deliberately. The aura of openness makes possible candid expressions of feelings and ideas. Even faulty communication does not lead immediately to retaliation, for others are not prone to presume malice on the offender's part, but instead "carry him;" compensate for his errors. Moreover, a lapse in communication is viewed not as an occasion for punishment but as an opportunity to learn from mistakes. Obviously, effective communication will do much to reinforce and enhance an existing trusting climate. But if communication performance begins to falter

repeatedly the trusting relationship may be jeopardized. People begin to wonder if the slip-ups are inadvertences or did the other fellow have something in mind. When self-fulfilling prophecies of intrigue and suspicion emerge, the organization may be in for trouble.[5]

Another function of open communication is to govern the balance of power in organizational operations. The mechanism of this function is described by John Gardner:

> I would lay it down as a basic principle of human organization that the individuals who hold the reins of power in any enterprise cannot trust themselves to be adequately self-critical. For those in power the danger of self-deception is very great, the danger of failing to see the problems or refusing to see them is ever-present. And the only protection is to create an atmosphere in which anyone can speak up. The most enlightened top executives are well aware of this. But I don't need to tell those readers who are below the loftiest level of management that even with enlightened executives a certain amount of prudence is useful. The Turks have a proverb that says, "The man who tells the truth should have one foot in the stirrup."[6]

What is the nature of the foundation upon which one can construct an organizational climate of open communication and trust? Such a climate can exist only when educational managers are men of personal and professional integrity. We use the word "integrity" to describe those educational managers who are:

1. Honest and straightforward in their interpersonal relationships.
2. Aware of their strengths and limitations; willing and eager to learn.
3. Consistent in their value dispositions, demonstrating reverence for human dignity in daily performance.
4. Flexible in their managerial style so that they can match style with situation without being opportunists; able to balance control with independence, authority with participation.

5. Morally courageous so they will maintain the independence of solitude during the pressures of dissent.

Impediments to the Development of Supportive Organizational Climates

The educational manager who encourages open and honest relationships can do much to promote a productive organization. Those who have lived in our school and college organizations know that trusting and supportive educational organizational climates are frequently oases in the desert of more dependent and autocratic climes. Why? One reason is that many educational managers attempt to resolve all conflict, or to cover it up, instead of trying to *manage* it. Another reason is that administrators often do not have the intellectual power or effectiveness in personal relationships to manage conflict creatively.

Trust and Conflict

If an educational manager permits and encourages the open expression of ideas in his organization, then the friction of these ideas rubbing together is certain to create some heat. The typical manager reaction is to don his fire hat and rush to the point of friction with bucket of water in hand. In the words of Richard C. Lonsdale:

> Some administrators, perhaps intolerant of ambiguity, seem bent on attempting to resolve all conflict or at least on covering it up. They miss the fact that some amount of social disorganization makes for stimulating relationships and positive change.[7]

And, Robert Chin observes:

> . . . The presence of tensions, stress or strain, and conflict within the system often are reacted to by people in the system as if they were shameful and must be done away with. Tension reduction, relief of stress and strain, and conflict resolution become the working goals of practitioners but sometimes at the price of overlooking the possibility of increasing tensions and conflict in order to facilitate creativity, innovation, and social change.[8]

In our determined effort to run a "tight ship," we tend to overlook the fact that some conflict and tension—when properly managed—are useful in the renewal of both the person and the organization. And renewal is essential to the continued viability of both individuals and organizations.

We are not here talking about the type of conflict which destroys both personal and institutional integrity and which may be generated solely to produce confusion and destruction. Indeed, the interpersonal and ideological conflicts which come to flower in our educational organizations may—if properly utilized and managed—prevent some of the larger conflicts.

Again we can look to the organizational literature to establish empirical bases for the positive contributions of conflict. But we do not need a flurry of footnotes to confirm the notion that crisis and challenge can make us stand on our tiptoes, call forth latent energy, produce innovative ideas, and loosen up rigid relationships. Change can then be effected more readily.

Trust and Competence

We have said that an organizational climate characterized by trust and open communication is certain to produce conflict. The challenge to the educational manager is to manage conflict so that the creative friction of ideas and personalities rubbing together does not escalate into a chaotic disruption of the entire educational community. The management of conflict is a task which calls for an intellectual and interpersonal engine of some power. That brings us to the second reason for the lack of trust and openness in educational organizations: some managers don't have this power! They are not tolerant and comfortable with open relationships because they lack confidence and security in their managerial competence. The probability of an incompetent manager generating an organizational climate of trust is about the same as that of "sneaking daybreak past a healthy rooster."

Consider this argument. If we encourage those with whom we work to share their opinions, feelings, and attitudes, then we had better be prepared to live with— and learn from—threats to our self-esteem and self-concept. We should keep our asbestos suit handy because we are sure to feel some of the heat given off in the conflict of open relationships. Our hypothetical asbestos suit, however, can take the form of a strong sense of personal identity. Not an identity that is rigid and inflexible, but one that can accept and evaluate feedback which may be incongruent with what we had in mind about ourselves.

The manager who has a strong sense of personal and professional identity, then, wants to learn more about himself. He values undistorted feedback, for this is how he builds his self-concept. To be sure that this feedback is undistorted, he must minimize the defensiveness of those on whom he depends. This defensiveness will not be reduced unless the organizational climate is one of open communication and a high degree of trust. And where do we find such climates? We find them where the responsible manager can sustain threats to his self-concept and the tension of occasional organizational conflict, and can encourage similar attitudes on the part of those with whom he works. That the competent educational manager must have a keen sense of identity is known to all who have successfully resolved conflicting role expectations and the press of competing ideas and interests.

Thus, the competent educational manager is one who is securely anchored by a strong sense of personal identity. But how does one develop this sense of identity? Interestingly, conflict can play an important role in identity formation. In his book *Human Aggression,* the British psychiatrist Anthony Storr states:

> In adult life, the aggressive drive which in childhood enabled
> the individual to break free of parental domination serves to
> preserve and define identity.[9]

In rushing about to smother and repress conflict in organizations, then, the educational manager only does himself a disservice, for in the crucible of conflict we can learn to define the boundaries of our personality. We learn what we can and cannot do. We learn our strengths and limitations. We learn also about those with whom we work and on whom we depend.

One of the authors recalls an occasion when a faculty member scheduled an appointment concerning a matter of salary. The faculty member forcefully pointed out that he was extremely dissatisfied with his salary and had offers of several jobs paying more than he was making. The composed and tactful response would have been to approach the matter in a round-about manner. However, the author chose a more aggressive tact and asked him if he would like a letter of recommendation for one of these other jobs.

There is a risk in such confrontations, but in this case the employee had a history of belligerence. Some resistance at the moment was justified. After the heated preliminaries, we were able to arrive at the core of his complaint. We talked for two hours. He learned that he did not have to engage in threats in order to discuss salary. He also learned that his salary was based on factors reasonably related to those of other faculty members with similar responsibilities and performance. The author learned that he had better exercise more self-control and pay more attention to salary structure. Out of the conflict emerged two individuals who had learned more about themselves and others.

A Matter of Balance

Experienced educational managers know well that there are few recipes and rules which can be applied to all organizational situations and decision-making problems. This is really the reason we are educational managers. There is an excitement in the day-to-day challenge of weighing the many dimensions of decision-making situations, of reconciling competing interests, of feeling the awesome responsibility for individual welfare, of agonizing over points of value, and of exercising power wisely. So we have not meant that the reader should accept what has been said uncritically and without careful reflection.

For example, we have said that the educational manager who is a man of integrity is honest and straightforward in his interpersonal relationships and encourages open communication. Does this mean that he has to tell all that he knows? No. There are times when too much communication can be disastrous for both individual and organizational welfare. We have indicated that the manager should try to develop an organizational climate of trust. Does this mean the absence of control and authority? Definitely not. For some members of the organization, independence and trust would just reinforce lethargic tendencies.

What of the emphasis on organizational conflict and tension? We have suggested that tension and conflict can have positive impact. Does this imply that the manager should move about with a big ladle to keep the organizational stew in a contant stir? No matter how positive the contribution of tension and conflict, all of us need respite from the press of our day-to-day affairs, some time to rest, reflect, and renew. And what of this business of developing personalities capable of sustaining threat to self-esteem and self-concept? Shall we assume that all persons are capable of sustaining such conflict? Such a point of view would be foolish indeed and in direct conflict with our knowledge of individual personality differences.

And, what about the stress of tension and conflict in terms of higher productivity? Again it is essential that we pay attention to the amount and conditions of stress.

In summary, the educational manager who wants to create a more viable and productive educational organization should know that productivity is increased by a climate of trust and independence. The development of trust, independence, and openness is more probable when there is opportunity for un-distorted and unfiltered information to flow all directions in the organizational structure. But the probability of such open communication is low unless the educational manager has suf-ficient personal integrity and professional compctence to with-stand the threats to his self-esteem and self-concept, and to see within the occasional organizational conflicts the potential for both individual and organizational renewal. The question, then, is whether those of us who are practicing educational managers can design and implement the type of organizational climate in which those with whom we work do not have to live with "one foot in the stirrup."

DISCUSSION QUESTIONS/LEARNING ACTIVITIES

1. Identify a situation in an educational organization in which conflict has served a useful and productive purpose.

2. What impact does collective negotiation have on the resolution of conflict in educational organizations?

3. This chapter suggests that there is a relationship between management style and the openness of communication in an organization. What is your reaction to this position? Give examples to support your position.

4. Search the literature to identify instruments that may be used to measure "organizational climate." Develop a plan for assessing the climate of a unit or institution and execute the plan if feasible.

5. Develop an attitude scale concerning organizational conflict. Administer the scale to friends or to practicing educational managers you know. Explore the relationships between their responses and their management style.

6. Does aggression serve any positive function? Review the work of Anthony Storr, Erich Fromm and others on this subject. Develop a paper to summarize what you find and its implications for management.

NOTES

1. Orin B. Graff and others, *Philosophic Theory and Practice in Educational Administration* (Belmont: Wadsworth, 1966), p. 304.

2. Rensis Likert, *New Patterns of Management* (New York: McGraw-Hill, 1960).

3. Chris Argyris, *Integrating the Individual and the Organization* (New York: John Wiley and Sons, 1964).

4. Douglas McGregor, *The Human Side of Enterprise* (New York: McGraw-Hill, 1960).

5. William V. Haney, *Communication and Organizational Behavior* (Homewood, Ill.: Richard Irwin, 1967), p. 13.

6. John W. Gardner, *No Easy Victories* (New York: Harper & Row, 1968), pp. 42-43.

7. Richard C. Lonsdale, "Maintaining the Organization in Dynamic Equilibrium," *Behavioral Science and Educational Administration: The Sixty-third Yearbook of the National Society for the Study of Education, Part II,* Daniel E. Griffiths, (ed.), (Chicago: University of Illinois Press, 1964), p. 154.

8. Robert Chin, "The Utility of System Models and Developmental Models for Practitioners," *The Planning of Change,* Warren G. Bennis et al., (eds.), (New York: Holt, Rinehart, and Winston, 1961), p. 204.

9. Anthony Storr, *Human Aggression* (New York: Antheneum, 1968), p. 57.

8
Decision Styles and Strategies

*The human understanding when it has once adopted
an opinion . . . draws all things else to support
and agree with it. And though there be a greater
number and weight of instances to be found on the
other side, yet these it either neglects or despises,
or else by some distinction sets aside and rejects;
in order that by this great and pernicious
predetermination the authority of its former
conclusion may remain inviolate.*

Francis Bacon

The history of scholarship in administration shows that at one
time our principal concern was for the "structural" elements of
administration and management. This period was followed by an
era in which the primary focus was on the "motivational" aspects of management. More recently the harmonizing theme
has been "decision making."

Contemporary writings on decision making range from earlier
book-length treatises such as *Design for Decision* by Irwin D. J.
Bross[1] to the sermonettes found in that delightful book *Up the
Organization* by Robert Townsend. The latter included this
exhortation:

> All decisions should be made as low as possible in the
> organization. The Charge of the Light Brigade was ordered
> by an officer who wasn't there looking at the terrain.
>
> There are two kinds of decisions: those that are expensive to
> change and those that are not. A decision to build the Edsel
> or Mustang (or locate your new factory in Orlando or
> Yakima) shouldn't be made hastily; nor without plenty of
> inputs from operating people and specialists.
>
> But the common or garden-variety decision—like when to
> have the cafeteria open for lunch or what brand of pencil to
> buy—should be made fast. No point in taking three weeks to

make a decision that can be made in three seconds—and corrected inexpensively if wrong. The whole organization may be out of business while you oscillate between baby blue or buffalo brown coffee cups.[2]

Between these two ends of the scholarship continuum there falls an array of articles and books, many of which present concepts of utility to the practicing administrator. It remains only for us to seize these concepts and bring them into a pattern of understanding so that we can put them to work in our everyday practice. If we accept the proposition that decision making and managing are synonymous, as Herbert A. Simon has done in *The New Science of Management Decision,*[3] then certainly our theme is a relevant one.

This chapter attempts to bring the theoretical aspects of contemporary scholarship on decision making into a meaningful interpretation for the educational manager. It will be convenient to order the discussion around questions that define decision-making behavior. Fundamentally, the educational manager, in common with other managers, confronts these questions:

1. What kinds of decisions are there and what kind am I facing (Typology of Decisions)?
2. What styles are available (Strategies and Styles for Decision Making)?
3. What personal and environmental variables can affect this decision (Environment of the Decision)?

A Typology of Decisions

Our premise here is that a recognition of decision types is fundamental to the selection of tools and strategies for making decisions. Thus, the first step in decision making is to define the character of the decision.

Positive and Negative Decisions

Over 30 years ago, Chester Barnard suggested that:

The fine art of executive decision consists in not deciding questions that are not now pertinent, in not deciding prematurely, in not making decisions that cannot be made effective, and in not making decisions that others should make.[4]

Barnard says that decisions are of two types, positive and negative. Positive decisions provoke action that commits the organization to some new goal or procedure for goal achievement. These are the kinds of decisions that usually come to mind as we ordinarily think about the business of educational management. The mental image provoked here is that of the energetic, charismatic manager who with a single "yea or nay" or with stroke of pen dedicates his organization to risky new ventures.

Yet Barnard reminds us that of equal importance and consequence are those negative decisions, decisions not to decide. The painful experience of ill-considered decisions teaches us to appreciate the wisdom of deferred action and stresses the notion that timing is an important element.

Programmed and Nonprogrammed Decisions

A second classification scheme widely heralded in the literature of decision making is "programmed and nonprogrammed" decisions, described by Simon as follows:

Decisions are programmed to the extent that they are repetitive and routine, to the extent that a definite procedure has been worked out for handling them so that they don't have to be treated *de novo* each time they occur . . .

Decisions are nonprogrammed to the extent that they are novel, unstructured, and consequential. There is no cut-and-dried method for handling the problem because it hasn't arisen before, or because its precise nature and structure are elusive or complex, or because it is so important that it deserves a custom tailored treatment.[5]

The purchasing officer who must decide whether he should "go out for bid" on new furniture may find that his decision is "programmed" to the extent that policy fixes the procedures for competitive purchase. The school superintendent who faces the question of whether his management structure should be decentralized and how this might be accomplished is not confronting a programmed decision. Consequences, not only of an educational character, but also of a political, economical, and social character, clearly mark his decision as a "nonprogrammed" one.

Said another way, the presence of policy will ordinarily identify programmed decisions, whereas nonprogrammed decisions will normally be those which represent exception to, or absence of, policy. Either way, the involvement of the educational manager is critical. One of the most important decisions to be made initially by the manager is to structure his organization for making "programmed" decisions so that he may devote his talent and energy to the "nonprogrammed decisions."

Routine, Problem Solving, and Innovative Decisions

Writing in *Management Decisions by Objectives,*[6] George S. Odiorne outlines a goal structure which permits the classification of decisions into three kinds—routine, problem solving, and innovative.

Routine decisions are those everyday, operational level decisions that keep the organization moving and ensure the maintenance of the status quo. The college admissions officer who admits or rejects a candidate in accordance with preprogrammed admissions policy may be said to be engaged in "routine" decisions. At a middle point on the decision-making continuum are those decisions dedicated to specific problem solving. Improvement and innovation decisions constitute the highest point of the continuum. These are the decisions which represent a planned and conscious effort to improve the way in which organizations operate.

Operational Decisions and Goal Setting Decisions

In *The Social Psychology of Organizations,*[7] Daniel Katz and Robert L. Kahn suggest four types of decisions:

1. Decisions which shape and define goals.
    (a) Sharpening and clarifying organizational purpose
    (b) Adding new goals and objectives
    (c) Shifting priorities among goals
    (d) Changing the mission of the organization

2. Decisions which specify procedures for goal attainment.
3. Decisions which apply policies to ongoing operations.
4. Decisions which are on-the-spot ad hoc decisions.

These authors suggest further that the proper concern of the executive should be with the first of these four types, after he has made provision for the other three. This is a point which we emphasized earlier. However, the educational manager with a proclivity for operation may devote himself to routine administration while his staff makes policy. The essence of the matter is well captured by Odiorne, as follows:

> Deans who should be generating grand schemes for new levels of education spend their days in endless rounds of administrative clucking at the actions of hostile and rebellious professionals.
>
> Research or educational administrators who should be encouraging creative projects spend their days engaged in form and procedures, checking locks on doors, inspecting the housekeeping, and auditing the books. The result is that such organizations are normally the worst managed to be found.[8]

Implications for Action

Too many managers at all levels in our schools and colleges are afflicted with management myopia. Their professional vision is severely limited by an aggravated case of nearsightedness. They spend most of their time fussing with the nuts and bolts of everyday operation and rarely stand back to ascertain where they are going. Schools and colleges managed with this kind of limited professional vision are prime candidates for educational disaster.

Contemporary organizational theorists stress that organizations must adapt to change in environment if they are to survive and to perform useful functions. Surely this is a timely observation.

Yet we all know educational managers whose entire commitment is to their inbasket. We need educational managers who will focus on those decisions which deal with the hard questions of educational direction. Thus, our primary focus should be on those decisions which are goal centered. But to bring the matter into proper balance, the manager cannot forget his obligation to establish effective vehicles for routine or programmed decisions as well. Herbert Simon put this point well:

> The executive's job involves not only making decisions himself, but also seeing that the organization, or that part of the organization which he directs, makes decisions effectively. The vast bulk of the decision making activity for which he is responsible is not his personal activity but the activity of his subordinates.[9]

Here is a clear lesson of involvement. While the educational manager must ensure that his perspective is sufficiently enlarged to account for the directions of his organization, he must not forget the need for harmonizing the theory of a decision and its application in practice. To put the matter more directly, we need to involve the man at the operational level, so that those at the highest decision-making levels do not forget the many decisions required to translate a policy into action. We do well to remember that it is generally easier to make decisions when someone else must bear the action consequences.

Strategies and Styles for Decision Making

As previously stated, the objective of our journey into the domain of decision making is to bring theoretical concepts into a perspective suitable for managers on the educational firing line. Preliminary mapping of the decision-making domain has been accomplished by discussion of the types of decisions which confront the educational manager. We turn now to a consideration of the strategies and styles which may be focused on the decision problem at hand.

Strategies for Decision Making

Much has been written about the processes of decision making. When the veneer of scholarship is stripped away, most of what has been written is simply a variant of the problem-solving process as originally outlined by John Dewey.

1. Immediate pressure on the decision maker (the felt difficulty).
2. Analysis of the decision problem and its context.
3. Search for alternative solutions to the problems.
4. Evaluation of consequences for each alternative and the selection of a final choice.

Odiorne has adjusted the decision-making process into six steps.

1. Have an objective mind.
2. Collect and organize all pertinent facts.
3. Identify the problem.
4. Develop possible solutions and alternatives.
5. Evaluate the possible solutions.
6. Set up controls and action plans to maximize the success of the decision.[10]

Certainly, the manager must gather all the facts relating to a decision. However, this is not the entire obligation of the effective decision maker. The character of decision reality is captured by Peter Drucker as he reminds us that:

> Most books on decision-making tell the reader: "First find the facts." But executives who make effective decisions know that one does not start with facts. One starts with opinions. These are, of course, nothing but untested hypotheses and, as such, are worthless unless tested against reality.[11]

Thus, feeling as well as fact plays an important role in decision making. The college business manager who knows the facts concerning the acquisition of property adjacent to his campus should be well attuned to the "feeling" associated with that decision problem.

Evaluation of solutions requires the additional application of value criteria and again points out the need for a sensitive philosophy and flexible style. The final step in the six activities suggested by Odiorne is a critical one—setting up action controls to ensure success of the decision. The history of decision making in education is filled with examples of decisions which emerged from the managerial gun with so little action that they fell harmlessly to the ground. An effective decision sequence must take into account those variables which can deflect our aim and thus ruin its desired effect.

The decision-making process is admittedly much more complex than the simple procedure outlined thus far. Can the firing-line manager find anything of value in this simple process? We believe he can, and suggest that he improve the power of his decision-making activity by:

1. Developing the clear goals that provide a target for decision-making activities.

2. Considering possible alternatives on their merit and not short circuiting the search by dismissing some because their implementation may cause administrative headaches.

3. Paying attention to the practical problems of translating a decision into action. Involving organizational personnel who have to live with the consequences of a decision.

4. Resisting the pressure for immediate action when the decision calls for a deliberate analysis of the problem.

Styles of Decision Making

The "Quick Draw" Artist. On one end of the style continuum is the "quick-draw" artist, the manager inclined to action and on-the-spot judgments. He aims to shoot the problem clean through on the first shot and move on to the next one. The merit of this style is that it satisfies those who desire action. It gives them the feeling that something has been done. Whether or not this action produces personal or organizational profit is lost in the satisfaction derived from the action itself.

To use this style for all decisions makes little sense. Deciding on what color chairs to put in the new cafeteria may well be decided by this style. But to spend several million dollars to purchase land needed for expansion should not be approached so lightly.

The Thinker. Rodin's famous statue of man thinking reminds us of the extended deliberation taken by some managers as they wrestle with decisions. The time taken is suggestive of wisdom, but in reality it may mask genuine confusion or ignorance. A school principal faced with a howling mob of students calling for a shutdown has little time for this style of decision making. The wisdom of his decision will be found in his philosophical commitment and quick analysis of the situation.

A Synthesis. In actual fact, practical decision making will involve elements of both styles. As the maestro's baton signals the mood of the music and moves to orchestrate the voices of the instruments in harmony and coordination, so should the decision style of the educational manager adapt to the demands of the decision situation. Some decisions should be approached with the deliberation of an andante and the quiet voice of pianissimo. Others require the speed of an allegro and the strong voice of triple forte.

Educational managers need to learn that decision style must be harmonized with the situation. We could gain much by the simple analysis of decisions which confront us each day. It is probably no exaggeration to say that some expensive man-hours are expended each day in our schools and colleges making decisions of little consequence, while the larger and more critical decisions wait outside the door. While the administrative cabinet agonizes over whether the parking curbs for staff should be painted red or green, incompetence in the classrooms goes unattended, outmoded curriculums remain unchanged, obsolete regulations and procedures continue to choke organizational health, and unimaginative allocation of previous resources continues. Just a little attention to the kinds of decision which occupy our attention can produce a new and higher plane of decision activity.

Environment of Decision

Our final concern is the environment of decision making. Our intention here is to examine the effect of three sets of environmental factors—structural, social-psychological, and cognitive.

Structural Variables

In *Integrating the Individual and the Organization*, Chris Argyris says:

> . . . organizations (of the future) will tend to vary the structures they use according to the kinds of decision that must be made. If one asks the individual in the organization of the future to see the company organizational chart, he will be asked "For what type of decision?"[12]

This comment makes clear what every practicing manager knows: the extent and type of involvement in decision making should match the character of the decision. Thus, the manager should be continually assessing the kinds of decisions to be made and designing differential modes of involvement.

Argyris has suggested a continuum of organizational involvement for different decision situations.[13] For example, centralized models with minimum involvement of organizational participants are appropriate when time is short, when decisions move the organization in previously established directions, or when decisions are routine and require little creative deliberation. This model is also proper when individuals in the organization are apathetic and do not seek involvement. It may also be appropriate when time and financial resources do not permit broad-based consultation.

Representative models of involvement may be credited to Rensis Likert,[14] who originated the "linking pin" concept in which a supervisor acts as a link between two groups. As an example, the role of a department chairman in a large university is one of linking his faculty and their concerns to members of the administrative staff and their concerns. The principal represents his faculty to community and to the school board or central staff. Under this model, the supervisor, or "link," provides opportunities for subordinates to discuss views on particular decisions and then presents the views to the next echelon. This model is most effective when some participation is desired but conditions do not permit total involvement.

A third model of decision involvement is functional in character. Participation in decision making is sought from those who have either the experience or expertise to assist in making a more effective decision. Decisions on the curriculum involve the faculty; those related to investments involve financial officers.

Another mode of functional decision making involves those who are unfamiliar with the problem. There are times when they, rather than the "experts," can produce creative solutions. In fact, there has been considerable study on how to free creative potential, bringing fresh views to both problem definition and solution. This approach is described by William J. J. Gordon in his book *Synectics.*[15] The tendency in our society to bifurcate the arts and the technical fields of science and engineering deprives decision makers of much creative talent in some technical problem solving. The synectics approach brings together diverse talents and prepares them, via a training program, to approach problems from a more open and divergent perspective.

Finally, we have the model of total involvement. Maximum participation is most effective when time and resources permit and when decision outcomes significantly affect organizational mission, work conditions, or specify how decisions within the organization are to be made. For example, it seems safe to say that maximum involvement is desired if a decision will affect tenure, teacher evaluation, or evaluation of new programs.

Social-Psychological Factors

In recent years, management theorists and scholars of organizational behavior have confirmed what the wise manager has known for a long while—man does not always behave rationally in the decision process. Bernard M. Bass has outlined four individual differences which can contribute to the nonlogical elements of the decision process.[16]

1. Differences in Psychological Set. Consider, for example, the perceptual set of a principal as he views a group of students converging on his office. What differences in decision expectation would be predicted for a principal who has just experienced an extended occupation of his office as compared to the one who just the previous week was visited by a group of students endorsing his administrative behavior?

2. Differences in Perspective. Interpretation of decision-making events may also be conditioned by the person's location in the organization. To a college faculty member, administrative attempts to measure teaching load might be received as a nuisance. To the insensitive college administrator, faculty members are incapable of vision beyond their disciplinary speciality. The executive director of the state coordinating board of higher education might think that college presidents are selfish perpetuators of institutional practice regardless of statewide validity or promise. And college presidents may wish that the executive director would develop some "institutional perspective" before he dabbles in statewide policy.

It is difficult to establish patterns of partnership in the decision-making process with such diversity in perspective. Yet an awareness of the diversity is certainly a first step in the right direction.

3. Differences in Personal Orientation. The psychological literature confirms the notion that dispositions differ and that these differences can contribute to role conflict between organizational function and individual personality. That this finding applies also to executive behavior is well captured by the writing of Zaleznik and others.[17] A self-oriented deputy superintendent, for example, might see a new computer-based information system as threatening to his job security. The interaction-oriented executive might be more concerned about the relations of those discussing the problem. And the task-oriented executive will likely be concerned about whether the computer will do the job specified. A lack of sensitivity to the interaction between managerial personality and the type of decision can surely complicate reactions to decision behavior.

4. Differences in Concern for Types of Organizational Problems. Also affecting the decision environment is the organizational concern of those making decisions. For example, a new vacation schedule and leave policy may be favorably received by the division director whose primary concern is with employee welfare, apathetically received by the manager unconcerned about vacation, and unfavorably received by the manager who is concerned about the financial cost.

As in the discussion of other factors related to the decision environment, we have not meant to suggest that these factors are in any way independent. They, too, will appear in a variety of combinations and further complicate the decision process.

Cognitive Factors

J. G. March and Herbert A. Simon originated the notion of "bounded rationality" by explaining that the real decision maker faces a number of environmental limitations. He has limited knowledge of alternative courses of action, the utility of alternatives, the probability of their occurrence, and their impact.

> The organizational and social environment in which the decision maker finds himself determines what consequences he will anticipate, what ones he will not; what alternatives he will consider, the ones he will ignore. In a theory of organization these variables cannot be treated as unexplained independent factors, but must themselves be determined and predicted by the theory . . . Choice is always experienced with respect to a limited approximate simplified "model" of the real situation.[18]

In the previous discussion of social-psychological factors, we have treated some of these variables. We conclude this section with an exploration of some psychological facets of the thought process. Our framework here is that suggested by Katz and Kahn.[19]

1. Determination of Thought by Position in the Social Space. This concept means that our knowledge, experience, attitudes, and judgment are largely affected by our position in organizational space. For example, in one of the most comprehensive papers on academic administration to come out recently, Terry Lunsford points out that college administrators and faculty members are living in increasingly divergent social worlds. He describes these consequences:

> A major effect of these changes has been to erode the informal relationships between administrators and faculty members, relationships which engendered and sustained the trust necessary for an easy exercise of administrative authority, and which muted the potential conflict between administrators and academics in the university of an earlier day. Radical shrinkage of informal contacts has also reduced the actual knowledge that administrators have of faculty and students—and *vice versa.*[20]

2. Indentification with Outside Reference Groups. The scholarly study of group processes confirms what we have informally recognized for a long while, that is, each of us is a member of many different reference groups; and our values and attitudes are affected by these group memberships. How group memberships affected the executive is well captured in the comments of Katz and Kahn.

> The information and values of these outside groups are given more weight than similar inputs from groups of lower status and power. The parochialism described above refers primarily to cognitive limitations due to the executive's way of life . . . There is rational justification for giving full consideration to power groups, since they may be helpful to the organization. The irrational element enters when they are consulted even though they have little to contribute in the way of knowledge or other help and where more lowly groups with relevant knowledge are ignored.[21]

In educational organizations, as in other organized activities, the division of labor and restricted communication associated with it reinforce the manager's isolation. Thus, perceptions of organizational environment—and associated decision problems—may be biased even before they encounter the filtering action of his frame of reference.

3. Projection of Attitudes and Values. In identifying with outside reference groups, we tend to see ourselves as being similar to others. Just the opposite occurs with projection, wherein we tend to see others as sharing our values and attitudes. The possibility of this cognitive limitation inhibiting effective decision making is high in the absence of factual information about the state of our organizations and the feelings of the different reference groups.

The message for the manager is clear. We need continual information inputs on the operational status of our organization and qualitative inputs which force us to take a fresh look at the attitudes and values of those groups in the organization.

4. Global or Undifferential Thinking. This factor represents the human tendency to oversimplify situations with which we are not totally familiar or where we are removed from the persons or place. From the point of view of educational management, this suggests that management style should be adapted to both organizational unit and persons within those units. How many principals tend to think of the faculty as a vague stereotyped group, attributing to them a single set of values and attitudes. The fact is, of course, that there is no such thing as "the faculty" with regard to attitudes and values. There are many different sub-groups. The same inaccuracy prevails when members of the faculty see all administrators as members of the mysterious and mistrustful group known to them as "the administration."

5. *Dichotomized Thinking.* Another form of cognitive limitation is the tendency to simplify decision situations into exclusive categories (you're either for or against me; there's a right way and a wrong way). This limitation denies access to alternatives which could bring about compromises. There is little inclination to explore compromises when we are disposed to engage in dichotomized thinking.

6. *Cognitive Nearsightedness.* The tendency in decision situations is to respond to the immediate, the visible, the pressing elements of the situation—often to the neglect of the far-reaching and critical impact of the decision. For example, the decision to build a new building of "x" square feet may meet the needs of this year's enrollment and the constraints of the capital budget. But, in the long run, a decision to construct a building which is inadequate the day you move in might be foolish.

7. *Oversimplified Notions of Causation.* Many problems of management are incorrectly analyzed because of the tendency to look for simplified causes of events. The now famous Hawthorne studies (see page 22) are good examples of the complexities of relationships between organizational welfare and the many personal and environmental variables.

Implications for Action

From this field of concepts, what can we harvest that will be of value? We find that:

1. Simply stated, the practicing manager should learn to adapt his involvement to the character of the decision.
2. In wrestling with different decisions, the administrator should know that his perceptions and those of others will be affected by past experience, organizational locus, differences in personality orientation, (i.e., per-

son-oriented versus task-oriented), and differences in concern for types of organizational problems.

3. In decision making, the administrators should confront those limitations of the thought processes which can inhibit effective decision thinking. We must resist tendencies to let our attitudes be shaped by other reference groups; to assign our attitudes and values to others; to engage in oversimplified notions of causation; to focus on the immediate impacts of the decision rather than long-range impacts; and to reject alternatives too soon.

Summary

Throughout this chapter, our goal has been to identify, and bring into a meaningful pattern, concepts that can help the educational manager improve the quality of his decision making. More effective decisions will emerge if the educational manager approaches decision making from a foundation of social and behavioral concepts rather than from a foundation of impulse, rules of thumb, tradition, or convention.

DISCUSSION QUESTIONS/LEARNING ACTIVITIES

1. To what extent do educational managers you know adapt decision style to situation? To what extent do they tend to deal with decisions in a characteristic fashion each time (the "thinker" approach or the "shoot-from-the-hip" approach)?

2. Do you believe the six-step decision process described by Odiorne is a good match with the reality of decision making in educational organizations? What part does opinion play in decision? Does opinion frequently hold sway over fact?

3. Someone has said that cabinet, council, and committee groups frequently spend long hours in fondling trivia and nibbling important issues to death. Can you think of examples that support this statement?

4. In this chapter we have listed several cognitive factors that affect decision making. These include the tendency to dichotomize decisions and overlook long-range consequences in the face of im-

mediate pressures. Give examples of actual decision actions that illustrate each of these factors.

5. This chapter outlines four models of decision involvement, from highly centralized approaches to complete involvement of all organization members. Give examples of actual decisions in educational organizations that represent appropriate application of each of the four models.

6. A number of simulation models are marketed as aids in examining the consequences of both short-range and planning decisions. In an analytical paper describe and evaluate one or more of these models.

NOTES

1. Irwin D. J. Bross, *Design for Decision* (New York: The Free Press, 1953).

2. Robert Townsend, *Up the Organization* (New York: Alfred Knopf, 1970).

3. Herbert A. Simon, *The New Science of Management Decision* (New York: Harper & Row, 1960), p. 1.

4. Chester I. Barnard, *The Functions of the Executive* (Cambridge: Harvard University Press, 1938), p. 194.

5. Herbert Simon, *The New Science,* pp. 58-59.

6. George S. Odiorne, *Management Decisions by Objectives* (Englewood Cliffs, N.J.: Prentice-Hall, 1969), pp. 20-23.

7. Daniel Katz and Robert L. Kahn, *The Social Psychology of Organizations* (New York: John Wiley and Sons, 1966), pp. 259-260.

8. Odiorne, *Management Decisions,* p. 136.

9. Simon, *The New Science,* p. 57.

10. Odiorne, *Management Decisions,* pp. 10-19.

11. Peter Drucker, *The Effective Executive* (New York: Harper & Row, 1967), p. 143.

12. Chris Argyris, *Integrating the Individual and the Organization* (New York: John Wiley and Sons, 1964), pp. 211-212.

13. Ibid., pp. 197-214.

14. Rensis Likert, *New Patterns of Management* (New York: McGraw-Hill, 1961).

15. William J. J. Gordon, *Synectics* (New York: Harper & Row, 1961).

16. Bernard M. Bass, *Organizational Psychology* (Boston: Allyn and Bacon, 1965), pp. 388-390.

17. Abraham Zaleznik, *Human Dilemmas of Leadership* (New York: Harper & Row, 1966), pp. 171-197.

18. J. G. March and Herbert A. Simon, *Organizations* (New York: John Wiley and Sons, 1958), p. 130.

19. Katz and Kahn, *The Social Psychology,* pp. 284-290.

20. Terry F. Lunsford, "Authority and Ideology in the Administered University," *The American Behavioral Scientist,* May-June 1968, p. 8.

21. Katz and Kahn, *The Social Psychology,* pp. 285-286.

9

Policy As A Management Tool

> *The only people who read policy manuals are*
> *goldbricks and martinets. The goldbricks memorize*
> *them so they can say (1) "That's not in this*
> *department," or (2) "It's against company policy."*
> *The martinets use the policy manual to confine,*
> *frustrate, punish, and eventually drive out of the*
> *organization every imaginative, creative,*
> *adventuresome woman and man.*
>
> Robert Townsend, *Up the Organization*

For years, observers of organizational life have dealt caustic verbal blows to policy makers and policy manuals. It has been said that the last act of a dying organization is to issue a greatly enlarged policy manual. Why, then, in the face of all this advice, do organizations continue to insist on the development and use of written policy guides and manuals? Formal policy must offer some advantage in organizational function.

Actually, policy is very much like any other management tool. It can be used or abused. And the abuse is more frequently related to the user than to the tool itself. Thus, the question is not necessarily whether one should have codified policy or not, but rather what policies are needed and how they can be put to work for more effective organizational function.

Policy Definition and Advantages

Justin G. Longenecker defines policy as a guide for management action.[1] Daniel Katz and Robert Kahn say that policy should include goals and objectives along with the procedures for achieving these goals.[2] William H. Newman defines policy as a "general plan of action that guides members of the enterprise in the conduct of its action."[3] James H. Donnelly,

Jr., and others suggest that policy making is a phase of the planning function of management; that policy is the principal instrument for reflecting the basic objectives of an organization; and that it is an important management tool for ensuring goal-oriented behavior.[4] In summary, policy describes the general goals of organizations—their reason for existence—and provides a guide to decision making for achievement of goals.

A frequent difficulty in policy writing is that of recognizing levels of policy. For example, Herbert Simon suggests that there should be three levels of policy in organizations.[5]

Legislative Policy—the ethical premises of management.
Management Policy—broad nonethical rules laid down by top management.
Working Policy—other rules of action and behavior.

As an illustration of the changing levels of abstraction, consider this. A university or a school system may state its intent to provide equal employment opportunity as a matter of legislative policy. As a matter of management policy, it may suggest that 50% of all new teachers hired during a year be members of minority groups. As a matter of working policy, it may prescribe the recruiting procedures that will lead to the realization of both management and legislative policy.

We should note that the level of abstraction is reduced as one begins to interpret policy in an organization—and therein lies some of our greatest difficulties and causes of abuse. It is one thing, for example, for a college governing board to promote the personnel policy that "all faculty shall have a weekly teaching load of at least 12 course hours or its equivalent" but quite another to interpret in an operational sense what "equivalent" means. A noble aim is expressed in the policy that teachers should be accessible to students, but quite a different motive may be given to the interpretation which says that all teachers must be in their offices until 4:30 p.m.

Similarly, it is possible for two educational organizations to have the same general policy for direction and quite different operating policies. For example, two colleges may give allegiance to the traditional goals of instruction, research, and service. But in the interpretation and implementation of that policy, one may decide to have an open admissions policy and another a selective admissions policy. Two urban school systems may subscribe to the same learning goals, with one being tightly centralized in its structure and operation and the other being totally decentralized. This is not unique to educational organizations. Business and industrial organizations can subscribe to the same directional policy but operate on widely divergent marketing and production policies.

Formal and Informal Policies

The policy expressed in a manual is just one manifestation of organizational beliefs and practices. In most organizations, and most certainly in educational organizations, there is an informal, implicit set of policies at work. They may not be in the book, but they are just as real and just as effective. For example, in one school system there was a formally published procedure for teachers to request transfers to another school. The policy described the criteria to be employed in such decisions and the forms and procedures as well. In actual practice, however, teachers were aware of "board feeling" that to request a transfer was equivalent to requesting assignment to lower regions of Hades.

In a university there was an institutional and formally published policy concerning change-of-course procedures, including the last dates to add and drop courses. However, there was considerable variance in the informal policy held by two different colleges of the university. In one college, student applications for change of course were treated impartially and with dispatch. In the other, the attitudes of the dean and faculty were such that a student hesitated to request any change of course, no matter what his reason. These two informal policies yielded interesting differences in student performance and failure rates—even though neither of them was formally described in university policy statements.

Advantages of Published Policies

Policy is basically designed to define organizational direction, to outline management intent, and to provide a guide for decision making. Some of the reasons for publishing policy in formal guides or manuals are:

1. *Delegation of Authority.* Policy amounts to an extension of managerial authority and thus permits decisions to be made without constant reference to higher authority.

2. *Efficiency in Decision Making.* If the routine and recurring decisions in an organization can be made on the basis of policy, the manager's time is not wasted in dealing with decisions which are repetitive.

3. *Economy of Management Effort.* Published policy should enable decisions, especially recurring ones, to be made deeper in the organization. Thus, the top-level educational manager should be freed to spend more of his time and energy in managing exceptions and in planning.

4. *Consistency and Equity in Decision Making.* Differing judgments can result in unequal treatment of employees, particularly in the critical areas of workload and rewards. Written policies should encourage equity and consistency of interpretation and application.

5. *Continuity and Training.* Procedures located only in the head of one who has left the organization are singularly hard to retrieve. An urban school system learned this lesson the hard way when its director of computers and administrative processing resigned. There was no documentation of either policy or procedure—which suggests that a new director was probably needed anyway. The absence of documentation created major disruptions in the system operation. These disruptions were at least tolerable until checks for teachers and administrators were one week late.

6. *Better Human Relations.* The human relations advantage may not be immediately apparent or even

believable, for it is in this area that policy most frequently seems abusive. However, policy should have a rationale and philosophical base that leads to a better understanding of reasons for actions and consequently better human relations.

The Manager and Policy Formation

Speaking of the role of the educational manager in policy development, Robert Hutchins said that the "administrator must accept a special responsibility for the discovery, clarification, definition, and proclamation of the [institution's] end. But he does not own the institution."[6] Roald F. Campbell and others pointed out that the "community, [governing board] and the chief administrator are directly involved with policy formation."[7] The nature of this interaction is described by Calvin Grieder, Truman Pierce and K. Forbis Jordan.

> . . . in policy making and legislation [by the governing board] there is a reciprocal relationship between the board and school personnel . . . If policies and legislation are to guide administration, those who make policies and legislate must know what administration requires. Hence policy making and legislation must be guided by what administration knows about the schools. The executive must point the way for those who have responsibility for education. Legislation alone can energize administration; administration alone can inform legislation.[8]

Certainly, the educational manager has responsibility for policy initiative at the level of "management" and "working" levels previously mentioned. We believe also that he has responsibility to work with governing agencies in the development of legislative policy. A leadership role in policy formation has a solid foundation in practice and is safely short of usurping a governing board's prerogative in establishing policy.

Policy Abuses and Dysfunctions

All of us are familiar with ways in which the policy tool is abused. A quick review of illustrative cases may suggest guidelines for improving the quality of policy.

Inadequate Concept of Policy Definition

Some policy manuals and guides are not policy at all but sets of procedures. Newman points out that the distinction between what is policy and what is procedure may well depend upon the perspective from which the content is viewed.[9] Occasionally, policy manuals may contain not only policy but job descriptions. The policy manual of one university devoted large portions to descriptions of major academic and administrative positions. There was no policy that dealt with the responsibilities of key academic personnel and major program areas. For example, there was no visible policy in such areas as promotion, tenure, evaluation, and curricular review. Yet one could easily find such vague and useless statements as "The Vice President for Academic Affairs coordinates with the other vice presidents on matters of concern to the University." What constituted "matters of concern" was a mystery insofar as the formal policy manual was concerned.

Development of Policy for Exceptions

Educational managers are prone to develop policy for handling exceptions rather than for general decision situations. Because managers deal so frequently with the exception, it is easy to develop policy on this basis. For example, the research director of a large university discovered that scientists in one of the research institutes were using the university computer for personal consulting work. Ignoring the fact that there were no abuses in the other six research bureaus and centers, the director published a policy which contained an elaborate set of control processes for any research use of the computer.

In reviewing financial records, the deputy superintendent in a large city school system found that a high school principal had equipped his school with an expensive laboratory in astronomy. That his high school had at best a mediocre program in basic physics did not stay this principal from investment in rather esoteric equipment. Infuriated at this exhibition of poor judgment, the deputy superintendent "promulgated" a systemwide policy requiring all purchase requisitions to be approved at the superintendent's level. This, of course, penalized the other principals who had exercised balanced judgment, convinced them that the superintendent's staff only existed to make life hard for them, and probably did little to correct the judgment of the single offender.

Policy as an Artificial Protector of Status

Educational organizations abound with policies that serve no productive function other than artificially protecting academic status. Colleges frequently limit maximum student load to 16 or 18 credit hours. The theory is that no student can do a respectable job with a greater load, especially in view of the rigor of college work. This premise ignores the fact that many bright and energetic students can well handle more course work, but they have to fight their way through policy and process just to earn the right to try. In reality, rigorous educational programs would make it improbable that a student would take more than eighteen hours. But we ensure the "status" of our program through a policy which prohibits students from trying to test the rigor of our programs. We thus produce a self-fulfilling prophecy; namely, that if we do not permit students to try we can be comfortable that indeed we do have rigorous, high quality programs.

This kind of policy nonsense is rampant in graduate programs as well. Ordinarily, advanced degree work should keep the full-time student adequately occupied. But we ensure an artificial rigor by policies which do not permit full-time students to hold jobs which require more than 15 to 20 hours a week of work. Of course, many intelligent and energetic students will carry full loads and moonlight jobs without our knowledge. They simply circumvent the policy.

No better example of this dysfunction exists than the matter of course prerequisite systems. Instead of defining prerequisites in terms of skills and knowledges required for successful performance, we define them in terms of other courses. In some disciplines, it is possible for a student to perform quite well without having had a parade of undergraduate courses in that discipline. But this is troublesome to our academic prestige, so we establish a pseudo prestige by insisting that a student show a long list of undergraduate hours before we will permit him to take graduate work.

Policy as a Punitive Tool

Senior colleges in one state decided that they should adopt some policy which would discourage the newly emerging community colleges from infringing on senior college prerogatives. That is, they did not want community colleges to offer more than two years of work or to entertain aspirations of becoming senior institutions. These senior institutions, therefore, promoted a policy which said that students could transfer no more than 60 course hours from a community college. On the surface, this would seem to serve exactly the purpose the senior institutions had in mind.

But this policy had a senseless effect on students. Here is a true illustration. One student, needing only a freshman level course in general biology to graduate, was told that he could not take the course in his hometown, regionally accredited community college. The student had already transferred 60 hours from a community college. Hence, he must travel 100 miles to attend a senior college for one class.

Use of Policy as a Substitute for Managerial Courage

In some institutions, policy is invoked as a substitute for managerial courage. Managers can develop a policy to get at a single offender without having to deal with him on a face-to-face basis. The principal in a large elementary school noticed that two teachers were habitually late. Rather than engage the issue head-on, she published a policy which required thal *all* teachers sign in when they arrive and sign out when they leave, thereby adding another control on the teacher who is on time and providing a challenge for the two late teachers, who within a week found a way to cheat the process.

Policy as a Substitute for Good Judgment

Policy can become a substitute for exercising good judgment in some situations. For example, in one university the official policy was that married women were not permitted to change their name of record unless they could present a notarized statement of the change. To accommodate students, one of the clerks in the registrar's office was a notary public. Students were treated to the curious process of being turned down by the first clerk, sent two steps left to get a notarized statement, and then moved back two steps with the notarized statement for the official change. Whatever the original philosophy behind this policy, it had clearly been bent all out of shape. Perhaps the reason for this kind of behavior is that no provision had been made for exceptions.

Newman suggests that policy flexibility can be ensured only when exceptions to policy can be made quickly enough to secure the benefit of concession.[10] If we cannot respond quickly, then we promote the kind of rigidity exemplified in these illustrations.

Inadequate Communication of Policy Rationale

A student enters the registrar's office of First Rate College and requests that a copy of his transfer work from Excel College (from which he had recently transferred) be sent to a prospective employer. The records clerk informs the student that college policy will not permit her to send a transcript from Excel, that she can only send a transcript from First Rate College. The student asks why. "Because it's against our policy," replies the records clerk, as she brandishes the college policy manual in her right hand. Exit one angered student.

Now just a moment taken to explain the rationale behind this policy would have helped everyone. The student might have been calmed if he could have understood that past abuses by students had caused registrars to agree not to release transcripts from other institutions because registrars have no way of knowing whether a student has outstanding obligations, especially financial ones, for which the record is being held. Unfortunately, however, no one ever bothered to explain this rationale to the records clerk; hence, she could hardly pass it on to the student.

That the communication of policy is important is emphasized by Longenecker:

> Policies often affect many who are not directly involved in their formulation. Managers at lower levels, for example, are expected to apply policies adopted at "headquarters." Employees including managerial personnel, are also expected to conform to policies regulating personal behavior. This creates a need for communication of policies to all personnel who are concerned with them.[11]

In the matter of educational policy, Robert L. Saunders and others have dealt with both the philosophical and research bases for communication and involvement in policy matters. They point out that more adequate decisions are likely to emerge when those affected by the policy are involved in its development.[12]

Overprescriptive Policy

There are organizational tasks of a technical and sensitive character which demand close adherence to prescribed rules. This may be especially the case in the flow of information and materials which must eventually be automated for computer analysis. However, we occasionally will write policy which is overprescriptive for the situation.

An electrician in a county school system was nearly electrocuted when he fell across a high voltage line and was saved only when a carpenter working nearby pulled the main power switch. With noble purpose, the director of plant published a policy which in effect said that maintenance personnel must work in pairs. It is at least questionable whether the policy increased safety, but there is no question that it had a negative effect on the efficiency of maintenance operations. Even the locksmith who is called over to unscramble the tumblers in the lock of the superintendent's door must take along his helper. Such a policy is clearly overprescriptive and, to emphasize a point previously made, a substitute for good judgment.

Maintenance of Obsolete Policy

In some of our educational organizations, expensive resources are wastefully spent because obsolete policies are still in effect.

The president of a small college was infuriated that two faculty members gave exams early in the summer term and left the campus two days before the term was over. Substituting policy for courage, he published a policy which in effect said that both instructors and students must be present on the day in which final exams were officially scheduled. Ten years later, two deans are following this policy to the letter with an interesting ritual. They have departments which give exams prior to regularly scheduled finals, and these exams serve as a final for the course. In each case, however, the instructors and students in these departments are required to show up at the time published in the schedule of classes. They sign a piece of paper which indicates that they were there and then leave.

Unfortunately, inattention to policy evaluation and revision is all too prevalent. Martin K. Starr has pointed out that lawyers and judges are employed full-time to provide interpretation of social policy and spend little time in evaluation of policy, which is a legislative and executive function. In organizations, however, these two obligations are entrusted to the manager. Thus, educational managers should not only attend to the interpretation of policy but remain vigilant to the need for policy evaluation and revision.[13]

Implications for Policy Action

What ideas can be extracted from these illustrations of policy abuses that will help educators improve the quality of policy performance? Let us structure these ideas into four phases of policy activity: policy development, policy communication, policy execution, and policy evaluation.

Policy Development

The first phase of policy activity is that of policy development. We need to keep several ideas before us. The first of these is to ensure that what we publish is indeed policy and not procedures or job descriptions. Policy should outline points of organizational direction, management intent, decision processes, and personnel involvement. Properly developed policy will in fact provide operational definitions of positions by describing the ways and means by which various positions are involved in decision processes.

A second concept to guide our action is recognizing that educational organizations are organic in nature. That is, parts of the organization are interdependent. Consequently, there are few matters of policy that do not have complex action roots. This idea suggests broadly based involvement in policy development.

Another notion is that some freedom is necessary for efficiency. We should not freeze the initiative and good judgment of effective personnel by publishing policy designed to control the actions of a small number of ineffective persons. Policy should not be used, therefore, as a punitive tool but as a tool to facilitate organizational operation.

Policy Communication

Policy communication is a cyclical process. It begins in the formulation phase, continues in the execution phase, and starts around again in the evaluation phase. There are a number of ideas to guide us. First, the effectiveness of a policy can hinge on a single word or phrase. The wording, style, and tone of written policies should receive rigorous review so that the policy will elicit positive feelings rather than hostile responses.

The responsibility for execution of policy often falls to those who have had little involvement in the policy development stage. We do well to remember that involvement builds allegiance. But it does more—it protects the quality of policy decisions. Successful policy action in more probable if those who are affected by policy actions are involved, or at least represented, in the development deliberations.

Finally, we will want to keep in mind that many managerial attempts to produce efficiency can have quite an opposite effect in action—especially if the philosophical base on which the policy is built is shaky or if the communication of policy rationale is poor. Thus, we can expect to see few instances in which it is sufficient to put a policy in action by the simple expedient of a memo or transmittal letter. The more thorough and personal policy communication can be made, the more likely we are to obtain the desired performance.

Policy Execution

Good policy will usually represent some compromise between philosophical elegance and administrative simplicity. There are some educational managers who have a hard time understanding this. But the simple truth is that the philosophical elegance of a policy has little value unless the intent of that policy can be translated into actions which are capable of being managed. This, of course, usually means that policy leaves some room for judgment. And well it should, because policy is not a substitute for good judgment on the firing line and it is not a substitute for managerial courage needed to deal with poor judgment. It is true that policy should encourage equity in the decision-making process; but if we attempt to write policy that will in action remove all initiative, risk taking, and judgment, we create organization automatons.

Policy Evaluation

No managerial tool reaches obsolescence so quickly as policy. Our system of policy activity should provide a means of ensuring continual review, evaluation, revision. The best judges of policy function are those who must use it. Our system should provide for feedback from the operating level and responsive action when a policy becomes obsolete. Managerial sensors should identify those times and places where existing policy has become dysfunctional and isolate those personnel who use policy as a recipe rather than a guide.

Summary

Policy is a management tool. It can be used to indicate organizational goals, value positions, and ways of achieving these goals. Policy can be both formal and implicit. Properly and artistically applied, policy can promote delegation of authority, efficiency and consistency in decision making, and better human relations. It can facilitate training and continuity of organizational functions.

But policy can be abused and frequently is. It can become a recipe rather than a guide, an excuse for inaction and poor judgment, a substitute for managerial courage, a punitive tool rather than a facilitating one. Policy can be narrowly conceived and poorly communicated.

The effective educational manager will develop an artistic touch in the use of policy as a management tool. He will work to formulate policy which is the product of broadly based thinking and involvement, combining philosophical soundness with administrative simplicity, balanced in prescription and freedom.

He will ensure that the intent of the policy is clearly communicated to all whom it will affect both during the formulation and implementation phases. Finally, he will ensure that feedback on the function of policy is solicited from those who place it in action.

DISCUSSION QUESTIONS/LEARNING ACTIVITIES

1. Give an example of a policy which was "philosophically elegant" but "administratively impractical." How could the policy have been revised to improve its practicality?

2. Select an educational organization known to you and identify one or more "informal" policies not found in policy documents but very influential in that organization.

3. Conduct an evaluative review of the policy system in an educational organization. Develop a check list of evaluation factors and use this check list to evaluate policy manuals and other documents, the procedures for development of policy.

4. Prepare an analytical paper on the "intent and impact" of a specific policy recently developed in an educational organization you know. Interview those responsible for its development, tracing both the reasons for the policy and the procedures used to develop the policy. Interview those on the "receiving" end of the policy, identifying their perceptions of reasons for the policy and how it was developed.

5. Can you think of a situation where a policy was developed in response to an "exceptional" case of behavior or circumstances?

6. Have one or more students in your school develop a "policy diary" in which the student lists those policies he encounters over a period of time and evaluates the impact of the policies.

NOTES

1. Justin G. Longenecker, *Principles of Management and Organizational Behavior* (Columbus, O.: Charles E. Merrill, 1969), p. 101.

2. Daniel Katz and Robert L. Kahn, *The Social Psychology of Organizations* (New York: John Wiley and Sons, 1966), p. 260.

3. William H. Newman, *Administrative Action: The Techniques of Organization and Management* (Englewood Cliffs, N.J.: Prentice-Hall, 1963), p. 40.

4. James H. Donnelly, Jr., James L. Gibson, and John M. Ivancevich, *Fundamentals of Management: Functions, Behaviors, Models* (Dallas: Business Publications, 1971), p. 72.

5. Herbert Simon, *Administrative Behavior* (New York: The Free Press, 1965), p. 59.

6. Robert M. Hutchins, "The Administrator," *The Works of The Mind,* Robert B. Heywood, (ed.), (Chicago: University of Chicago Press, 1947), p. 151.

7. Roald F. Campbell, Edwin M. Bridges, John E. Corbally, Jr., Raphael O. Nystrand and John A. Ramseyer, *Introduction to Educational Administration,* 4th edition, (Boston: Allyn and Bacon, 1971).

8. Calvin Grieder, Truman M. Pierce, and K. Forbis Jordan, *Public School Administration,* 3rd edition, (New York: The Ronald Press, 1961), p. 127.

9. Newman, *Administrative Action,* p. 42.

10. Ibid., p. 44.

11. Longenecker, *Principles of Management,* p. 107.

12. Robert L. Saunders, Ray C. Phillips, and Harold P. Johnson, *A Theory of Educational Leadership* (Columbus, O.: Charles E. Merrill, 1966), pp. 84-85.

13. Martin K. Starr, *Management: A Modern Approach* (New York: Harcourt, Brace, Jovanovich, 1971), p. 429.

10
Managing Information Systems

*The evidence so far indicates widespread
unpreparedness to absorb more than a fraction of the
accumulated data, or to make truly effective use
of new communications and information techniques.
It indicates greater preoccupation with quantity
rather than with quality—more concern with
amassing new facts than with developing the structure
and relationships that will convert them to meaningful
information.*

*Until there is more general awareness of these
shortcomings, until plans and policies are better
organized to harness the new technology, we shall
face the possibility of a breakdown rather than a
breakthrough in our management of public and
private enterprises.*

Robert Sarnoff, *Machine Design* Magazine

Information is a resource to be managed. It is a resource as real and as valuable, perhaps more so, than plant and finance. There is evidence, in the literature and conversation of educational management, of growing interest in information and the tools we use to manage it. One can find increasing reference to planning and management systems; and the term management information systems (MIS) elicits a variety of cognitive and visceral reactions, depending upon one's experience with the applied meaning of the term. Advice from econometricians, operations researchers, systems analysts, and computer specialists who champion the design and application of information systems arrives simultaneously with advice from humanists. Such diversity of counsel can cause the practicing manager to vacillate between character calibration and protective pussyfooting, between the desire to quantify every educational activity and the desire to quantify nothing. Thus, the educational manager stands with information tools ready, not sure how and when they should be applied.

There is certainly nothing inherently wrong with our interest in planning and management information systems. But when we attempt to apply these tools to problems of educational management without balanced perspective, then we are vulnerable not only to disappointment but to less effective performance in our organizations as well.

For example, as a part of its management information complex, a large urban school system established an office of facilities planning. This office employed several clerks and one professional administrator with a doctorate in the maintenance of an elaborate set of PERT *(Program Review and Evaluation Technique)* charts for building construction. The apparent sophistication was impressive. That there was little congruence between the network of charts and the real construction world out in the community did not stay the expenditure of resources on this application of a new decision and information tool. The tool was sophisticated all right, but its practical value to the superintendent was zero. The expenditure of administrative resources on this office produced no useful output. This is an example of educators' attempts to utilize new management information tools without obtaining productive output—where educational management has become the tool of its tools.

Officials of a medium-size university decided to discard a modest but effective data processing unit utilizing second generation equipment (computer terminology for transistor-based equipment) for a new arrangement of hardware (computer word for equipment and machines). The new hardware was third generation equipment, had cost the university six times more than the old equipment, and was supposed to enable development of a total information system. Unfortunately, the sophistication of the equipment was not matched by investment in people to utilize it. After two years, the president of the university continues to take visitors down to see the magnificent new machine busily pecking out erroneous reports at a speed four times faster than the old one. Apparently, no one has bothered to evaluate the promises on which the machine was purchased or to realize that an information system requires man-machine compatibility.

Consider still a further example. In the central office of a small but relatively affluent city school district, one can find an elaborate array of four massive rotary files, each electronically controlled to deliver the "A" or "Z" files at the touch of a fingertip. This technology is part of an information system package recently marketed to the district superintendent. How often are these files used? On a busy day, one might see two of the four units accessed once in every hour.

Do these illustrations suggest that educational managers should abandon attempts to utilize information systems and associated technology? Not at all! Let's look for a moment at the other side of the situation—illustrations of effective planning and use of information systems.

A large state university recently found its student information system useful in drawing attention to discrepancies in student aptitude and performance. An analysis of several thousand freshman aptitude scores—made possible by computer power and a well-designed student information system—revealed that the freshman class ranked well above the national average on mathematics aptitude. However, an analysis of performance in freshman year mathematics courses revealed that more than 50% of the freshmen were failing these courses. Although such information does not identify cause and effect relationships, it certainly does provide an information base for raising some interesting questions. In this case, the information led to the installation of a mathematics placement program and the restructuring of the freshman math curriculum.

In another case with positive outcome, the finance information system of a city school district provided data which revealed that large sums of cash were lying idle in isolated accounts. This knowledge permitted the director of finance to make short-term investments and thus realize additional income for the system.

The personnel information system of a medium-size private university enabled the vice president for academic affairs to discover inequities in faculty workload among several departments. In this case, the availability of information confirmed isolated feedback flowing to the vice president and enabled him to provide additional staffing money to a hard pressed department. By means of the same information system, this vice president discovered that another department had doubled the size of its faculty at a time when its student enrollment had dropped by one third. These data also proved to be useful at budget time.

In some offices, the telephone is the most advanced piece of information technology to be found; but it can be a powerful one. The deputy superintendent for student services in a large urban school system found that the installation of a rotating call director system of phones enabled his office to deliver better service at two-thirds the previous clerical cost.

We have emphasized that management tools can be used or abused. We have emphasized also that the abuse is more frequently traced to the user than to the tool itself. The major source of problems in the effective application of any kind of information system is the *failure to adapt the system to the people who will use it*. This problem is treated caustically by Harold Hodgkinson.

> Into this context we now wish to add a word from our sponsors, the proponents of planning and management systems. These are the people who brought us those great hits, the TFX fighter, the M-16 rifle, and the C5A cargo plane. Some critics have actually had the nerve to criticize these miracles of industrial precision just because the fighter crashes, the rifle jams, and the C5A regularly loses wheels on takeoffs and landings, the wings crack, and the engines occasionally fall off while the plane is standing still.

> What the critics do not see is that the systems which produced these objects are perfection itself. The system assumes that rational information will be handled in a rational way. Nobody plays politics. If a department is shown to be unnecessary according to the management system, the individuals simply accept the judgment and quietly leave to seek employment elsewhere. The fact that the General Accounting Office now says that 45 major military systems will cost the government $35.2 billion more than the original contracts called for, cannot be attributed to the management systems; the systems are perfect; it's the people who were at fault. This is why systems people are being

> referred to as the new utopians, and also why OEO is giving
> up their commitment to Management Information Systems
> (MIS).
>
> A word of advice. A management information system is a
> *means,* not an end in itself. After use, however, the systems
> have a funny way of becoming an end and may become just
> as hard to change as the patterns they replaced. The system
> you purchase may be beautiful, rational, and precise, but it
> may produce TFX fighters and M-16 rifles. And don't expect
> *it* will make decisions for *you.*[1]

Hodgkinson counsels a deliberate and balanced approach to
the design and use of information systems. While it is clearly
inappropriate for the educational manager to become a slave to
his information systems, there is another facet of the management
attitude which can be just as unfortunate.

Some educational managers may become so apprehensive of
information systems, especially computer-based systems, that
they may shun them entirely. The patterned flicker of console
lights, the quiet spinning of tape drives, the irregular chatter of
disk access arms, and the staccato peck of high speed printers
create an aura of mystery. The manager may be so intimidated by
the esoteric language and the mystery of mathematics that he does
not mobilize his managerial courage and curiosity to discover
that the fundamental ideas behind most information and systems
tools can be mastered by anyone willing to invest the effort. In the
remainder of this chapter we will explore how management
information systems can be put to work for more effective
performance by educational managers at all levels.

Management Information Systems: Elements and Characteristics

First, what is meant by the phrase "management information
system." Start with the last word of the phrase, the word
"system." Most of us are surrounded by different kinds of systems
each day, but never stop to think of these relationships as systems.
We have electrical systems, heating and cooling systems, and
physiological systems. A system is a collection of *input* elements
(information, persons, records, electric current) which are

processed or transformed to generate some type of *output* or product.Figure 6 shows the basic idea. Any kind of system has some type of *input* which is *processed* to produce some kind of *output*. A *feedback* loop adjusts the function of the system according to the quality and quantity of output.

Figure 6. Diagram of System Concept

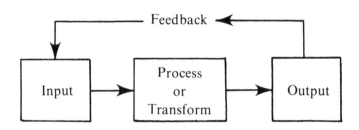

Now to the second word of the concept. An *information system* is one in which the elements of the system are information elements. The *input information* (dollars, test scores, ages, square feet) are *processed* (averaged, added, ranked, listed) to produce some type of *output information* (a report of average IQ score by age and sex, for example). Thus, a pupil or student information system may take as input certain basic data elements (age, sex, and aptitude scores) and by certain processes (classification and averaging) produce an information output (average mathematics aptitude for male and female students). A facilities information system may take as information input (net square feet, room type) and by processes (addition and classification) provide us with a report (total square feet for office space and classroom space). A personnel information system may take as input data elements (personnel-classification, age, tenure-status) and process these input elements to provide a display of the number of teachers with and without tenure by sex and age.

A "management information system" is a cluster of information systems which provide data for planning and decision making. Harry J. Hartley has defined an MIS as "any formal system of procedures established to provide useful symbolic information in the planning and decision processes . . . ”[2] Another writer has defined an MIS as an “organized method of providing past, present, and projection information relating to internal operations and external intelligence. It supports the planning, control, and operational function of an organization by furnishing uniform information in the proper time frame to assist the decision maker.”[3]

In essence, then, a management information system is a cluster of component information systems which provide information for decision functions. In educational settings, an MIS is usually conceived to include the following subsystems:

> Student or Pupil Information System
> Facilities and Plant Information System
> Financial Information System
> Personnel and Staff Information System
> Program Information System.

And, as the management information system is itself compounded of several subsystems as listed above, each of these also can be broken into small components. This, by the way, is another characteristic of systems thinking: any system is always part of some larger system. For example, the student information system in a college may have several subsystems to handle advising, admission, records, and registration. The financial information system for a school district may have subsystems for payroll, for revenue and expenditure accounting, and for budgeting.

Another useful way of looking at management information systems is in terms of the kinds of decisions to which we may apply them. Figure 7 permits us to examine this relationship. The relationship depicted suggests that an information system should be compounded of two parts, internal or “institutional intelligence” and external or “environmental intelligence.” In other words, educational managers need information both about the organization itself and about the environment—political, social, economic—of which it is a part. Thus, the superintendent and his staff may need a larger input of environmental intelligence for strategic decision making than will the principal, who may

find his greatest need for institutional information so that he can
wisely direct operations at his level.

Figure 7. Levels of Decision and Information Mix

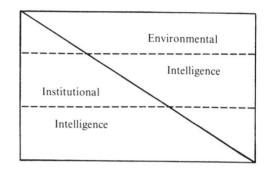

Strategic and Planning
Decisions

Environmental

Control and Evaluation
Decisions

Intelligence

Institutional

Operating Decisions

Intelligence

Another useful way of looking at the structure of information
systems is shown in Figure 8. The diagram shows three levels
of information. At the base of the structure are those information systems essential to the control and operating decisions
required in daily activities. At the next level are management
information systems. They link the first level information systems, generate analytic reports of a more complex character,
and permit the decision maker to review interaction of resource patterns. Finally, we have planning and management
systems which permit simulation decision work.

The principal difference between the third and second level
systems is that the second level management information systems
provide historical data, whereas the planning and management
systems provide a view of the variance of resource needs based on
variance of internal and external inputs.

The true test of any management information system is that it
delivers information in the right *form*, at the right *time*, and to the
right *person*. To what extent are management information
systems meeting this test? There are sharp differences of opinion.
In a paper appearing in the *Harvard Business Review*, John
Deardon indicated that "MIS is a Mirage,"[4] that a truly
integrated and comprehensive information system does not and

probably will not exist in most organized enterprise—unless we have some kind of information superman to help us out. However, Deardon was taken to task a short time later by Terrance Hanold who said that an MIS is essential to modern organizations.[5] The differences between the two may be a

Figure 8. Hierarchy of Information Systems*

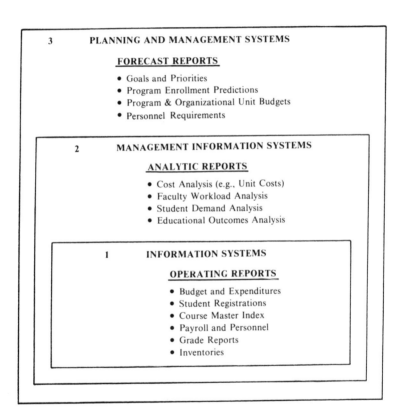

*Bernard S. Sheehan, *Report One - Western Canadian Universities Task Force on Information Needs and Systems,* University of Calgary, Alberta, Canada, November, 1972.

matter of definition. Some think of MIS as a single system, fully integrated and comprehensive. If this definition is accepted, then Deardon is probably right. Few organizations, including colleges and schools, are this far along. Most schools and colleges are still struggling to get their component information systems working and are far short of beginning the complex work of integrating the various component systems.

But if we view an MIS as a cluster of information systems from which we extract data for strategic, control, and operating decisions, then Hanold may be correct. This we are beginning to accomplish. Many of the decisions now being made in our schools and colleges have required at least some integrating of component systems. Some of the costing and modeling work being done has resulted from our ability to integrate data from two or more systems.

One of our problems is that we often allow information systems and computer systems to become entangled. Peter Drucker has taken the stance that:

> At present, the computer is the greatest possible obstacle to management information because everybody has been using it to produce tons of paper. Now psychology tells us that the one sure way to shut off all perception is to flood the sense with stimuli. That's why the manager with reams of paper on his desk is hopelessly uninformed. That's why it's important to exploit the computer's ability to give us only the information we want—nothing else.[6]

Now perhaps it is time to return to the test with which we began this discussion. Whether you have a single system or a cluster of systems, whether you have an information system that is computer-based or not, the final test of the effectiveness of your system is whether it delivers to you the form of information you need at the right time.

Those educational managers not operating at the president's or superintendent's level may wonder what management information has to do with their work. In educational organizations, those educational managers close to the firing line are seldom involved in the full use of information systems. What college, for example, has taken the trouble to acquaint its deans and department chairmen—who spend most of the money in

Readers interested in exploring both theory and practice in contemporary MIS development will find the following resources of value.

For Higher Education—*(The work of the national Center for Higher Education Management Systems of the Western Interstate Commission for Higher Education is especially central. See the commission publications among others below.)*

Robert A. Huff, *Focus on MIS: A Report on the WICHE-ACE Higher Education Management Information Systems Seminar, Washington, D.C. April 24-26, 1969,* (Boulder, Colorado, Western Interstate Commission for Higher Education, October, 1969).

Objectives and Guidelines of the WICHE Management Information Systems Program (Boulder, Colorado, Management Information Systems Program, Eastern Interstate Commission for Higher Education, May, 1969).

Ben Lawrence, George Weathersby, and Virginia W. Patterson, (eds.), *Outputs of Higher Education: Their Identification, Measurement, and Evaluation* (Boulder, Colorado, Western Interstate Commission for Higher Education, July, 1970).

Systems for Measuring and Reporting the Resources and Activities of Colleges and Universities, (R. J. Henle-Project Coordinator), National Science Foundation, June, 1965.

Francis E. Rourke and Glenn E. Brooks, *The Managerial Revolution in Higher Education* (Baltimore: Johns Hopkins Press, 1966).

Charles B. Johnson and William G. Katzenmeyer, *Management Information Systems in Higher Education: The State of the Art* (Durham: Duke University Press, 1969).

For Public Schools—

William H. Curtis, (ed.), *Educational Resources Management System: A Special Report Prepared by the ASBO Research Staff on a Planning, Programming-Budgeting, Evaluating System* (Chicago: Research Corporation of the Association of School Business Officials, 1971).

Harry J. Hartley, Educational Planning-Programming-Budgeting: A Systems Approach (Englewood Cliffs, N.J.: Prentice-Hall, 1968).

Frank W. Banghart, *Educational Systems Analysis* (London: Macmillan, 1969).

Gary M. Andrew and Ronald E. Moir, *Information-Decision Systems in Education* (Itasca, Illinois: F. E. Peacock, 1970).

For General Reference—

*Planning Series-*Parts I, II, III Reprints from *Harvard Business Review* (Cambridge: Harvard Business Review).

*Management Information Series-*Parts I, II, Reprints from *Harvard Business Review* (Cambridge: Harvard Business Review).

*Computer Management Series-*Parts I, II, Reprints from *Harvard Business Review* (Cambridge: Harvard Business Review).

Don Q. Matthews, *The Design of the Management Information System* (Princeton: Auerbach, 1971).

Norman Enger, *Putting MIS to Work* (American Management Association, 1969).

Morton F. Meltzer, *The Information Imperative* (American Management Association, 1971).

colleges—with modern management information systems? And how many principals are acquainted with the use of management information in their daily work?

Some college presidents and school superintendents have already discovered how embarrassing it is for city councils, governors, legislatures, and coordinating boards to know more about their operation than they themselves do. Consequently, these presidents and superintendents are beginning to develop and utilize information systems extensively. Soon, department chairmen in colleges and principals in schools will make the same discovery—that they need to know as much about their own operation as the college president and superintendent do respectively. And this will be a healthy turn of affairs, for the balanced application of information to educational decisions should lead to more effective management at all levels.

Thus, a system of management information is not an idea to be applied only at the top of educational organizations. Any educational manager who hopes to fulfill his responsibilities—for goal setting and planning, for resource acquisition and allocation, for resource organization, and for evaluation—needs organized and timely information. Now these information needs may be met as a part of the total organizational information system or the individual manager may have to design his own. One does not need to be trained as a systems analyst to ask such fundamental questions as these:

- What do I need to know about programs, personnel, finances, material, and students? When do I need this information and in what form?
- How and where do I initially get these facts and figures and how do I keep them up to date?
- What processing steps are required to translate facts and figures into a usable form?

These same questions may be viewed from a more technical perspective as suggested by Roger Kaufman who relates the questions to be answered in educational systems analysis and the steps in the analysis process (see Figure 9). But as Kaufman also points out, "a systems approach as described here is nothing more than an application of logical problem solving that allows the educator to plan and manage relevant and practical educational outcomes."[7]

The educational manager may find that a professional trained in systems analysis and computer concepts can assist him in the work of developing an information system. But systems analysts and computer specialists are not manager substitutes! Analysts are not always the best judges of the purposes for which information is needed and utilized. Furthermore, any change in purpose of a goal is likely to frustrate the systems analyst for, as John McManama has observed, "systems engineers become so mesmerized by the sheer elegance of a neat system that no one is allowed to mess things up by suggesting that the objectives are no longer meaningful."[8] The manager should be in the best position—if he will take the time—to define the kinds of information needed for the decisions he has to make.

Figure 9.   The Questions To Be Answered in a System Analysis and Their Relation to the Steps of Performing That Analysis.[9]

Questions to Be Answered by an Educational System Analysis	Steps in an Educational System Analysis
Where are we going and how do we know when we've arrived?	Determine mission objectives and performance requirements.
What are the things that will keep us from where we're going and how do we eliminate them?	Determine and reconcile constraints.
What are the major milestones along the way to where we're going?	Determine mission profile.
What are the "things" that must be done to get to each milestone?	Perform function and analysis.
Of what specific tasks are the "things" composed?	Perform task analysis.
What are the possible ways of getting the "things" done?	Perform methods-means analysis.

Moreover, the theme of this book is that there is an artistry in educational management, that the educational manager understands not only the technical actions required to get something done but the meaning and human implications behind these actions. In educational environments, many activities of value do not reveal an immediate utility. Leaving the management of information resources solely to those "mesmerized by systems" can lead to interesting and bizarre results. Consider, for example, this paraphrased narrative of a symphony concert submitted by a systems analyst with limited sensitivity:

> For considerable periods the three oboe players had nothing to do. By spreading their work over the whole of the concert, peaks of activity could be reduced, and the number reduced to one.

> The entire violin section of twenty frequently were playing identical notes, clearly an unnecessary duplication. The staff of this section should be reduced. If a larger volume of sound is required, electronic amplifiers may be employed.

> Considerable effort was absorbed in the execution of thirty-second notes in some of the more technical passages. A frivolous refinement, these may be rounded to sixteenth notes. Of course, this would render the passages more simple and permit the use of trainees and lower grade operatives—a move of obvious efficiency.

> Further, there was extensive repetition of some musical passages. No useful purpose is served by repeating on the woodwinds a theme already well handled by the strings. A careful pruning of the redundant passages could reduce the concert time of two hours and thirty minutes to forty-five minutes. And then, of course, there would also be no need for an intermission, thus reducing the rental time for the concert hall.[10]

As shown in Figure 10, a well designed information system (small and simple or large and complex) will be adapted to the kinds of operating, evaluating, and planning decisions which are made at each level. This kind of activity is just as common to the school principal and college department chairman as it is to the superintendent or president. Indeed it may be more important, for resources are *expended* and utilized not by presidents and superintendents but by those managers closer to faculty and students.

Figure 10. Information and Educational Decisions

Historical	Information Profiles	Assist the Educational Manager in Making	Operating	Decisions
Current			Evaluation & Control	
Projected			Strategic Planning	

Information in Action: Benefits

Some educational managers may not be seized with optimism about the contribution of information systems to the management of activities for which they are responsible. Others, however, will choose to venture into the field, and some will find themselves forced into information systems development as a protective measure. Whatever the reason for entry, the educational manager who gets involved in information systems design and application can expect both benefits and frustrations. Here are some of the benefits.

The Clarification of Goals

One of the merits of "systems" thinking is that it forces the manager to focus on "output," and this type of thinking should lead to clarification of goals. How can we decide what type of information we need in our system until we have first defined what we are trying to accomplish? Only then will we have a much clearer notion of the planning, evaluation, and operational information needs. Thus, any manager who struggles to design an information system which he can put into action, whether it be simple or complex, will discover that an important payoff of his struggle will be a clarification of goals. This is a worthwhile benefit.

There is a marked tendency for some managers to want to gather reams of data. Unfortunately, this tendency is encouraged by computer power. This kind of information aspiration also generates application forms, questionnaires, and other data collection devices that look like some kind of application for a top secret security clearance. "Tell me all you know, but be sure to write between the dotted lines and in the spaces provided." When confronted with the question of how he plans to use particular information, this manager is more embarrassed than the researcher who has a beautiful questionnaire but doesn't yet know what his research problem is. Evasion of the question proceeds frequently with the comment that "it would be nice to have that piece of information." This is shallow camouflage for the fact that the manager does not have in mind a clear set of goals and information output needs.

The Clarification of Process

Another benefit of information systems planning is that the manager will become more knowledgeable of people-process interactions in his operations. One surprised fiscal officer for a school district found that processing of invoices in his office required ten different clerical checks. The installation of an automated accounting system isolated the useless complexity and resulted in the assignment of clerical personnel to more critical areas. An academic dean in a medium-size college discovered that his psychology department and sociology department were both teaching a similar course in social psychology and were even using the same text. Now this might not have been so bad, except his student information system revealed that enrollments in the two courses had averaged less than ten per section over the past five years.

The Advantages of Preciseness

One of the concepts that the manager learns quickly, especially if an information system is computer-based, is the advantage of being precise. Even the most competent of systems analysts and computer programmers can do little with ill-conceived requests for services. In fact, analysts may end up making decisions which should not be theirs to make and thus accepting blame which is also not theirs. Computer specialists describe this problem with the acronym GIGO—"garbage in, garbage out." The principal who requests a list of tenured faculty for his school and finds that the list sent out from the district data processing office is in social security sequence will know next time to be more precise and request the list in alpha order. This leads us to still another benefit.

The Merits of Documentation

Some educational managers have a habit of carrying policies and procedures around in their heads. A far better habit is documentation of both process and policy. Documentation tells us:

1. What information outputs are to be furnished in what form, to whom, and at what time.
2. What information inputs are required from whom, in what form, and at what time.
3. What is to be done (process) to input data in order to produce outputs.

Documentation of systems interactions reduces personnel conflict, provides a public record of the scope of information services, ensures a careful and considered approach to information systems development, assists in the training of new personnel, and protects operation stability against the loss of personnel.

The Benefits of Planning

The importance of planning for both present and anticipated needs will also be learned in designing an information system. Because any kind of system, and especially a computer-based system, tends to become formalized and complex, and because it usually requires heavy investment of human energy and money, it also tends to become difficult to change. In the past, the focus has been on the development of individual information systems within a school or college, or even within a given department or unit. Thus, the typical approach has been to build an automated student information system or pupil accounting system and then proceed to accounting, payroll, and finance. Now we are busy building interfaces (common boundaries) among these systems so that we can get even more helpful data. The complexity of such system interactions are overwhelming. Even in the simplest information system, it is easy to overlook the effect of some seemingly insignificant change.

One frustrated director of school finance discovered that 2,000 monthly checks went out in error because a programmer had made changes in the budget system that caused an error in the payroll system. A few more gray hairs were added to the collection of a college registrar who found out that 12,000 grade reports had been mailed moments before the data processing manager informed him that all GPA's were wrong because a programmer had corrected the new retention policy but inadvertently forgot to change a variable in the grade processing system.

The Pleasures of Simplicity

An important lesson to be learned from the design and implementation of information systems is the value of being simple. Remember that any information system requires information input. We may do what we will after the data are in. But if the input data are inaccurate or incomplete, what we do with the data is irrelevant. Students, faculty, and educational managers are inundated with documents, each of which falsely assumes that the instructions will be read with care and understanding. Information systems should be designed so that input modes are simple as possible, that instructions are clear and minimal, and that follow-up edit and control checks are the order of the day.

The Necessity of Broad Perspectives

Finally, the design and application of an information system will probably lead the manager to broader perspectives of organizational function. In designing systems he will learn that many information variables are interacting. The educational manager able to see beyond the walls of his own organizational unit is likely to make more informed decisions.

Summary Reflections

1. Information is an organizational resource. The effective management of that resource is as important an obligation as the management of human and fiscal resources.

2. The manager must be prepared to spend time and energy on information systems design. Systems analysts, computer specialists, and quantitative decision specialists may be useful in design and application, but they are not manager substitutes.

3. An information system should be parsimonious; that is, it should deliver to the manager only that information useful in planning, control, and operating decisions. It should not inundate the manager with reams of useless output.

4. Information systems can be designed and applied with technology as simple and commonplace as the telephone. However, computers provide powerful storage and analytical power which may be essential for the development of complex information systems in our educational organizations.

5. An information system is not just a collection of equipment and procedures. It is complete only when these components are interfaced with the people who will use the information.

6. Information systems are a means and not an end. Managers should guard against becoming the tool of their tools, against persons becoming slaves of machines and systems.

7. Information systems should be evaluated for performance. The ultimate effectiveness test of the information system is that it delivers information in the right form at the right time to the right person. A further test is that the system frees the manager for more person-to-person contact rather than spending his time in managing the system.

8. Some provision is required in the information system not only for operating data from within the organization but for external data and input as well.

9. A management information system is a cluster of information components that provide managers with information for strategic, control and evaluation, and operating decisions.

10. Middle-level managers (principals, supervisors, department chairmen, deans) should be encouraged to put information systems to work in improving management performance.

DISCUSSION QUESTIONS/LEARNING ACTIVITIES

1. Can you think of an office in which operations could become more effective and efficient by rearrangement of that simple item of information technology—the telephone. Develop a staff study that shows how this could be done.

2. To what extent is a "management information system" usually thought of as containing only internal or institutional intelligence as compared to both that and external or environmental intelligence?

3. Give an example of an educational organization or office acquiring a piece of information management technology in the name of sophistication rather than effectiveness.

4. Interview specialists for planning and/or information systems on a school system or college staff to (a) determine when and why their positions were established, (b) what their roles and responsibilities are, and (c) how they evaluate their contribution to the work of the organization.

5. Develop a case study report that describes events leading to the purchase or lease of a new computer. Describe the persons involved in the decision, the activities of the company marketing the computer, the criteria used to evaluate the proposal, and the match between promises and performance over time.

6. One benefit of information is the capability to plan. There is a good deal of current debate on the benefits and limitations of educational planning. Develop a paper on "The Utility of Planning Products in Education" or "A Definition of Educational Planning."

NOTES

1. Harold L. Hodgkinson, "Goal Setting and Evaluation," *Planning and Management Practices in Higher Education: Promise or Dilemma?* (Proceedings of the National Forum on New Planning and Management Practices in Higher Education held in Denver, January 26-28, 1972), Richard Millard, Karen Sweeney, Nancy Eklund, (eds.), Educational Commission of the States, 1972, pp. 36-37.

2. Harry J. Hartley, *Educational Planning-Programming-Budgeting: A Systems Approach* (Englewood Cliffs, N.J.: Prentice-Hall, 1968), pp. 37-38.

3. Walter Kenneron, "MIS Universe," *Data Management,* September 1970.

4. John Deardon, "MIS is a Mirage," *Harvard Business Review,* January-February 1972, pp. 90-99.

5. Terrance Hanold, "An Executive View of MIS," *Datamation,* November 1972, pp. 65-71.

6. Peter Drucker, *Technology, Management and Society* (New York: Harper & Row, 1970), p. 174.

7. Roger A. Kaufman, *Educational System Planning* (Englewood Cliffs, N.J.: Prentice-Hall, 1972), p. 23.

8. John McManama, *Systems Analysis for Effective School Administration* (Wedy Nyack, New York: Parker, 1971), p. 176.

9. Kaufman, *Educational System Planning,* p. 22.

10. Sharvey Umbeck, "Better Management in Higher Education," *Vital Speeches Of The Day,* December 1, 1970, p. 103.

11
Evaluating Personnel Performance

> *Performance appraisal will always exist and always
> has. In any group a person's performance will be
> judged in some way by others. Employees and
> managers recognize differences among their peers,
> and they expect their own differences in performance
> likewise to be recognized . . . Appraisal systems
> are, therefore, necessary for strategic and tactical
> planning, motivation, communication, and equity.*
> Keith Davis, *Human Behavior at Work*

One of the marks of a profession is that practice is performed on
the basis of an accepted body of knowledge. Another requisite
is that the membership has sufficient autonomy to determine
minimal requirements for admission and to deny admission when
these requirements are not met. Closely related to both of these
requisites are the *ability and willingness* of the profession to
evaluate the performance of its constituent members. In most
instances, professional groups have the authority and display the
willingness to define acceptable standards of ethical conduct, to
prescribe minimal levels of performance, and to expel members
who fail to perform at the prescribed level.

The medical and legal professions have achieved autonomy
and exercised it more than education has. Although these powers
have been used by medicine and law at the admission level more
than at the performance level, it is not uncommon for a fully-
licensed member of these professions to be expelled when his
performance has been judged unsatisfactory, or in violation of
accepted ethics. While in expelled status, he is forbidden by law to
practice his art and skill.

When evaluated according to these criteria, education does not
hold a status comparable to medicine and law. It is often argued
that a major reason why this is true is that America's educators
are also "public servants." This means that in most states a board

of education or a college governing board (both usually composed primarily, if not exclusively, of laymen) control both the admission and expulsion of teachers and administrators. This oft-used explanation breaks down easily. Note that a county health officer is also a "public servant." He cannot, however, maintain that employment (in which he is responsible to a governing body somewhat comparable to a county school board) unless he has been found *by the medical profession* to be qualified to practice medicine. Moreover, if subsequently found *by the profession* to be practicing unsatisfactorily, he cannot continue in his practice as a doctor under any circumstances. Thus, the "public service" factor is not a valid explanation, certainly not the sole one, of why education does not hold true professional status. The answer must be found elsewhere.

While the individual educational manager cannot solve the problem of admission to and expulsion from the practice of education, he does have considerable freedom—and an obligation—to work with various groups such as professional associations, state regulatory agencies and governing boards to bring about better policies and practices in performance evaluation.

To do this will not be easy, especially if our past record is any indication. It is probably true, as often charged, that the educational manager has performed least well in performance evaluation. At the present time, of all the responsibilities of the educational manager, assigned or assumed, the evaluation of performance seems to be carried out least satisfactorily. Why? Certainly all the shortcomings—and they are numerous in this instance—are not of his own making. Several limitations, often seen as insurmountable barriers, are imposed from without. Therefore, the educational manager should know what some of these barriers are and how they might be lowered or even removed.

Barriers to Effective Evaluation of Performance

The Intangibility of Teaching Outcomes

When we talk about performance in education, we are talking first about teaching performance. Teachers constitute the overwhelming majority of the members of the educational enterprise and their work is the heart of the total mission. Effective performance in teaching, contrary to effectiveness in other fields such as salesmanship, engineering, production, or athletics, is extremely difficult to measure. There are several reasons why this is true. One is that teaching outcomes are difficult to assess. For example, there is no real consensus on the desired products of education. Are they changed behavior, achievement of factual information, changed attitudes, development of certain values, and development of certain skills? Are they creativity, independence, dependence, conformity, or an inquiring mind?

In analyzing the uniqueness of the educational organization and its administration, Roald Campbell and others developed six continua upon which schools can be analyzed and compared to other types of organizations. One continuum is "difficulty of appraisal," which is the heart of our concern here. Campbell illustrates the simplicity of evaluating performance in sales organizations where effectiveness correlates closely with production and sales volume. At the other end of the continuum (most difficult) they place the church, where evaluation is dependent upon recognition of both inner and outer changes. They place the school next to the church. The school, they contend, must be concerned with changes in behavior.

> The school (in contrast) must be concerned with change in behavior, to use behavior in a broad sense. The change may involve knowledge, skills or attitudes—all of which presumably influence behavior itself, but these changes are not immediately or easily perceptible. Often procedures or instruments have to be devised to measure change. But even when special instruments or procedures are used students may, particularly in short-run evaluation, give what they believe to be appropriate responses. Sustained changes in behavior can be determined only over a period of years and by the accumulation of evidence from many sources. Obviously the delay and the complexity of the evidence make useful feedback to the school for the purpose of revising practices most difficult.[1]

Lack of Consensus Regarding Goals and Purposes

Evaluation of teaching can be achieved only in terms of objectives: that is, the extent to which the learner learns what he is expected to learn. The difficulty here is that even after more than a century of public education, there exists no real consensus regarding the purposes of schools and colleges. Attempts by national commissions and other organizations notwithstanding, mere observation indicates a wide variety of purposes being sought throughout the nation, within a state, within a given school system or college, and even within a given institution itself. To an alarmingly high degree, the purposes of education are determined by the extent to which the individual teacher convinces the learner to accept and work toward his purposes.

Resistance by Educators

Another obstacle has been the steadfast resistance of many teachers, both in public schools and colleges, to agree upon procedures by which they ought to be evaluated. For that matter, even the idea of being evaluated is often rejected. Much of the discussion surrounding this point has revolved around the idea of merit pay and its alleged unworkability, and the widely publicized inference that administrators are not capable of evaluating teaching—nor in position to do so. The suggestion that teaching should be evaluated by several individuals and groups, including the teacher himself, his colleagues, his students and their parents, has generally been rejected outright.

This steadfast and effective resistance by teacher organizations has resulted in continued utilization of external and generally less effective procedures for determining promotions, raises, and changes in assignments. Years of teaching experience and level of formal preparation have remained the primary means for determining these matters, for teachers, administrators and other support personnel. A more rigorous selection and retention posture is now possible. It remains to be seen whether evaluation policies adopted will in fact result in only the best remaining with the profession.

The Latency of Educational Outcomes

Perhaps the most serious obstacle blocking the development of effective evaluation of teaching performance is the fact that many—perhaps even the most important—outcomes of teaching are latent in nature. They do not reveal themselves fully until years after the learner has left the formal school setting. If schools genuinely strive to help students achieve long-range and broad goals, such as learning to learn, developing saleable skills that will stand the test of time, becoming well adjusted and productive members of a complex and changing society, and becoming good parents and neighbors, then a true evaluation of teaching effectiveness must wait until the students function as adults in our society. This line of reasoning suggests that only interim evaluative judgments can be made while the student is in school and that a true evaluation must logically await his performance as a graduate. It also suggests that perhaps more attention should be given to evaluation in terms of process rather than outcome. More about this later.

Lack of Agreement on the Role of the Teacher

Just as there exists no consensus on the purposes of education, a similar problem exists in respect to the teacher's role. What function or functions should he perform? As Olivero has pointed out, this shortcoming necessarily complicates and restricts efforts to define "good teaching." Olivero states:

> As one reviews teaching literature, one is struck by the differences of opinion about what constitutes good teaching. The teacher, regardless of grade level or subject area, traditionally has been expected to perform many functions, but little has been accomplished toward defining those specific behavioral patterns expected from teachers. This is one reason why some educators can grade the same teaching act anywhere from unsatisfactory to outstanding. Obviously, before any type of judgment can be made, individuals need to reach some sort of agreement on the behaviors being observed.[2]

It follows, then, that until a working consensus is reached on the above point we will experience difficulty in designing and validating instruments to judge teacher performance. Some colleges and schools, however, have realized some success in defining and agreeing upon certain specific behaviors teachers and administrators are expected to exhibit and have developed instruments which help measure the extent to which the behaviors are followed. They have provided a foundation upon which to move toward higher levels of competence. This development will be covered in more detail in a following section which describes promising practices and developments leading us toward better programs of performance evaluation.

Thus, a number of barriers probably have held up progress in solving the historical problem of evaluating performance in education. It is tempting at this point to conclude that no workable plan can be developed and simply to accept this as one of the several inherent limitations of the educational enterprise. However, taking an honest and optimistic view, we acknowledge several current developments and a few in the formative stage which offer reasons for renewed efforts to solve this age-old problem.

Brief analyses of several such developments appear in the discussion to follow, along with an attempt to relate them to performance evaluation and the role of the educational manager in this process.

Recent Developments Which Will Affect
Performance Evaluation

Taking the optimistic view that adequate systems of performance evaluation can be developed, and coupling it with the rather clear mandate that education must become increasingly accountable, let us now look at some of the developments which may prove helpful in establishing such systems.

Increased Involvement of, and Responsibility Assigned to, Educators

As a result of strong pressures applied by practicing educators, several states have passed legislation establishing professional practices boards—a definite move in the direction of professionalizing education. Typically these boards are assigned responsibility from the state board of education. In most instances, educators are eligible to serve on these boards, enabling the profession to have a greater voice in determining its own affairs, or, as some prefer to describe it, policing and controlling its ranks. A study of these legislative enactments, however, reveals that most often the dimension of performance evaluation is missing.

A few plans, however, assign the professional practices commissions (composed solely of educators) authority and responsibility for developing through the teaching profession certain criteria for evaluating professional practices, including ethical *and professional* performance. Unfortunately, however, performance criteria have not been forthcoming. With reference to the matter of genuine control, the commissions are not autonomous in that they do not have the power to expel. They can only investigate and recommend action to the state boards of education and governmental agencies. They are not dealing with the factor of performance evaluation in a fundamental way.

Improved Statements of Educational Objectives and Goals

On the scene now is a pervasive movement which may well have a profound effect on both the improvement of performance and on the ability of educational managers to know when effective performance is taking place. This movement is mosaic at the moment but several dimensions germane to this chapter are apparent.

Real progress is being made, for example, in identifying instructional objectives, developing instructional strategies to help students achieve those objectives, and developing procedures and tools which permit students, teachers and parents to know when, and the extent to which, the objectives are achieved. Contributions by Bloom,[3] and others, are helping educators to understand that what is taught can be organized into a hierarchy, or ladder of content and objectives. Bloom exhorts educators to view educational objectives in terms of a classification system (taxonomy) of educational objectives, ranging from memory (least difficult) to evaluation (most difficult). This illustration refers only to objectives in the cognitive domain. Similar illustrations could be made in the other two domains (affective and psychomotor) where hierarchies have been established also. In fact, a publication by Armstrong, Cornell, Kramer, and Roberson entitled *The Development and Evaluation of Behavioral Objectives*[4] provides good illustrations of instruments which can be used to measure behavior in each of these instructional domains.

Mager adds additional insight through his identification of three basic components of teaching. He has formulated them into three questions: (1) what is it that we must teach? (2) how will we know when we have taught it? and (3) what materials and procedures will work best to teach what we wish to teach? Mager also describes how objectives can be specified and sets forth an "orientation that views goal specification as an unavoidable practical problem requiring hardheaded solutions."[5]

Sanders,[6] in a publication based on the earlier work of Bloom, has extended the concept of taxonomy and behavioral objectives and applied it to classroom teaching. Each of Bloom's seven levels of thinking is dissected, evaluated, and put into workable form by illustrating how each level can be utilized in the teaching process, through the technique of questioning.

Lessinger,[7] addressing the larger question of accountability, extends the concept even further by advocating the use of performance contracts to ensure clarity in the identification and achievement of objectives. This, he argues, is necessary if educational accountability is to be successfully implemented. Lessinger argues that just as an air conditioning contractor can promise a specific reduction in inside temperature below that outside and has an instrument (a thermometer) with which it can be determined if the promise has been met, so can a school principal promise that by their 12th birthday all children attending his school will be able to read 200 words per minute with 90% accuracy. He contends further that a specified measuring device (a test) can be used on each child's 12th birthday to determine if the promise (contract) has been met. Both the contractor and the educational manager, Lessinger points out, can employ alternative procedures and equipment when and if the approaches they employ fail to produce the desired results (promises).

Education seems to be moving to the point where goals can be defined, instructional process can be dissected, and measuring devices can be employed which will tell when and to what degree objectives have been achieved.

Formalization of New and More Viable Instructional Strategies

Currently on the scene, also, are attempts to analyze teaching performance and to organize resources, human and material, in such a way that different people perform different roles according to designated assignments and competencies. A number of promising practices fall within this broad movement, such as team teaching, micro-teaching, individualized instruction, prescriptive teaching, and the exciting new concept being referred to most often as staff differentiation, a concept borrowed from the medical profession which describes a team of organizational specialists performing different and complementary roles. For example, in the medical profession, nurses, medical technicians, and doctors form a team to deliver health care service. In education, teachers, teaching aides, learning resource specialists, and others combine to provide learning services. Staff differentiation may be the most promising of the several developments identified above.

The basis for this optimistic view is the potential that staff differentiation has for removing one of the big stumbling blocks to performance analysis; that is, that since the typical teacher has been expected to perform most, if not all, of the separate and component parts of the total teaching process, there has been no practical way to differentiate between those components performed well and those performed poorly. Stated another way, for many teachers poor performance in some aspects of the total teaching process counteracts and nullifies effective performance in others, resulting in overall mediocrity despite outstanding performance in one or more components.

There is little doubt that a trend is developing toward the use of staff differentiation. In fact, the *Educational Innovator's Guide* includes staff differentiation as one of 40 innovations which are believed to have an impact on education today. The relevance of this innovation to the thrust of this section can be seen in the following statement from this publication:

> As one reflects on the proposed advantages of differentiated staffing and its criticisms, problems, and pitfalls, he is struck by the great number of arguments that can be presented both for and against it. One of the more baffling problems is that of determining the different levels of responsibility, assigning duties to the respective levels, and assessing the competencies required. Many teachers fear that the plan is a scheme to exploit them. Conservative administrators are reluctant to involve teachers in policy development and decision-making. Others see better staff utilization as another significant move toward providing an education appropriate to each child. The advocates of the plan insist that it will put teaching on the broad, though bumpy, road to becoming a true profession.[8]

We concur that certain problems are yet to be solved before staff differentiation can make its maximum impact. This is probably true with respect to all innovations. However, staff differentiation is a current development which supports our thesis that effective systems for evaluating performance in education can be developed.

The matter of philosophy and purpose must be articulated as a prerequisite to staff differentiation. For the same reason, decisions must be made regarding what is to be taught and how it is to be taught prior to the decision to differentiate staff.

Observation and study suggest that considerable attention is being given to these prior questions, and that the teaching process is becoming better understood in terms of its components and dimensions. Among a large number of experimental programs designed to research this contention are those federally funded programs concerned with teaching teachers of teachers, popularly known as TTT. These programs have good potential for making significant contributions to both a better understanding of the teaching process and redefinitions of it. The TTT program at Auburn University,[9] for example, has identified four basic components of the teaching role, or, as viewed in that program, four teacher roles. These roles are:

1. The teacher as diagnostician
2. The teacher as a facilitator of learning
3. The teacher as interactor
4. The teacher as innovator.

The four roles have been defined behaviorally, followed by the specification of desired behavior and the development of learning modules, using a modified Comfield Model.

Other developments could be cited which are common knowledge among educators who stay abreast of the current scene. The purpose of this section, however, is merely to offer evidence that there is reason for optimism, that education may at last be well on the road toward having a philosophical and scientific base upon which performance evaluation can be carried on effectively and routinely.

But up to this point this chapter has dealt with reasons why performance evaluation is highly desirable, why progress has been slow (with detrimental results), and the notion that more productive days may be ahead for both the person whose performance needs to be evaluated and for the educational manager who must see that it gets done.

Let us turn now to what is going on by way of performance evaluation. The following section describes, analyzes, and to some extent, evaluates practices employed by educational managers as they are currently attempting to carry out this important, but as yet quite unscientific, process.

Currently Used Evaluation Systems

Current performance evaluation procedures are approached from three angles: (1) the individual's preparation for his role, including formal and informal preparation and experience; (2) the identification and promulgation of practices, behaviors, and characteristics valued most highly by the employing organization and how well the individual meets these expectations; and (3) the impact made on persons or programs by performance of the individual being evaluated.

We will discuss each of these approaches, which may be viewed respectively as input, process, and output. We'll try to identify the strengths and limitations of each; to illustrate practices and procedures often seen in operation; to probe the potential each has for furthering the cause of effective evaluation of performance; and to identify pitfalls, cautions and safeguards about which we feel the educational manager should be aware as he employs one or more of these three approaches.

Evaluation Before the Fact - Preparation and Experience

State agencies, usually state boards of education, have established a formalized and legalized system of certification now in effect in all 50 states. Certification is an attempt to assure that all licensed (certificated) educators have met minimal requirements judged by other educators (but ratified by state boards of education) to be positively correlated to effective performance.

Certificates are available (and uniformly required for licensed practice in most states) in dozens of performance areas ranging from teacher aides in a few states all the way to certificates for school administrative personnel. The latter, in some states, requires six years of college or university study. "Successful experience" and additional college preparation are required in most states to keep a certificate valid. Evidence of "successful experience," however, is often no more than poorly monitored and routinely offered evidence of actual employment for the number of years required.

Completion of a four-year preparation program is required in most states. Certification for some support personnel, such as administrators and counselors, requires formal course work beyond the bachelor's degree level. Many states offer certification on four levels ranging from the baccalaureate to the doctorate.

The belief that persons entering the profession of education should have completed a preparation program designed specifically for the performance area in which he is certificated has been strengthened by other agencies, such as the eight regional accrediting associations which use this factor, along with others, in ascertaining a school's eligibility for accreditation.

These associations often are more stringent than state and local boards of education, often requiring, for example, the certificate be in the area of the holder's assigned responsibility. (Mere possession of a valid certificate in any of the several fields is permitted in many states). Some states, which offer certificates according to the level of formal preparation, reward the educator and the system financially in proportion to the level and type of preparation.

Three systems of reciprocity (NCATE, NASDEC, and Interstate) are currently operative. They permit a certificated teacher, administrator, or counselor, to receive similar certificates in any of the participating states.

Colleges and universities do not utilize the certification process, except for a few junior colleges which are governed by local school boards (K-14 or 1-14), but similar benefits and safeguards are realized through the action of accrediting agencies. Some agencies are concerned with general evaluations (as in the case of the eight regional accrediting agencies) while others concentrate on specific program areas (as in the case of the NCATE for teacher education and ECPD for the preparation of engineers).

Accepted practices in colleges and universities have for some time placed heavy credence on the terminal degree and on delineating requirements (competencies) necessary for the various professional ranks. The large supply of doctorate-holders, the fact that professors are relatively mobile, and the number of professors who gained extraordinary experiences as a result of the many externally funded programs in the 1960s provide the educational manager with unequaled opportunities for artistic uses of the selection, retention, and reward system.

Thus, a rather good foundation (legal and educational) has been laid for admitting to the profession only those persons who have completed approved preparation programs for their areas, for maintaining their assignments in areas for which they were prepared, and, to some extent, for assuring that their preparation remains current. This system has served education well and is continually improving. It is not, however, being fully utilized in many instances and at best falls short of qualifying as a truly viable system of performance evaluation. This limitation notwithstanding, there are several ways the basic concept can be extended and made more viable by the educational manager and by governing boards, which will at the same time pay additional dividends and also move the profession closer to performance evaluation.

Educational managers can urge their governing boards to adopt policies that exceed the requirements of state departments and accrediting agencies. For example, a school system might require that all of its high school social science teachers complete a master's degree with a grade point average of no less than B. The system might require that additional college courses, or their equivalent, be completed, in the field of specialization or in agreed upon areas, at least every three years. (The math teacher who has had no formal study of number theory since the advent of "New Math" may be seriously incompetent in this respect). Teachers of foreign languages may be rewarded for, or even required to, travel or live a short time in a country which uses the language.

Public school systems could require all new teachers who hold no degree higher than the bachelor's to complete a master's degree as a condition of contract renewal after a certain time, say five years. Colleges and universities might develop a similar policy for all new teachers without the terminal degree.

Greater attention could be given to the experience factor. For example, judgments could be made (for purposes of salary, promotion, and tenure attainment) on a more systematic basis than is usually the case. More evidence of satisfactory performance in the present assignment could be required.

Another possibility for improved use of this basic approach is in the realm of informal preparation—a program of prescribed continuing education. The educational manager might prescribe, in conjunction with a teacher, learning and growth activities for the teacher based on their collective assessment of his needs, or areas where deficiencies are found to exist and where additional competence seems to be highly desirable.

Correlating opportunities for professional growth with evaluative assessments suggests that it would be well to move now toward the second basic approach currently used to evaluate teaching performance.

Evaluation in Terms of Practices, Behaviors, Attitudes and Characteristics Valued by the Organization

The approach described in the preceding section is rather far removed from any direct linkage between performance and impact, or "cause and effect." This section describes a second approach, one which establishes a closer linkage and which offers greater promise for success in the effort to appraise performance effectively. This approach is a process whereby an organization (1) identifies and makes public those practices, behaviors, attitudes (and sometimes personal characteristics) it considers indicative of satisfactory performance; (2) establishes some system for ascertaining the extent to which educators possess these characteristics and for monitoring behavior in terms of these stated expectations; (3) determines how much congruence exists between these two factors; and (4) finds ways for achieving better congruence, granting or withholding rewards (salary, promotion, tenure), or in some cases moving for dismissal.

The artistic educational manager can combine these four interrelated and sequential processes into a workable system of performance evaluation. When the system is developed properly, the educational manager can act with confidence and effectiveness in evaluating performance. He must still recognize that the process is short of the ultimate objective of linking performance with impact on the learner.

Let us look now at some ways these processes may be employed with maximum effectiveness, what experience tells us about effective implementation, and some intricacies involved. Then we will identify precautions and pitfalls which the educational manager should guard against.

A recent report by the Educational Research Service[10] states that about 93% of all school systems in the country employ some form of performance evaluation. Data are unavailable regarding the degree of usage in colleges and universities, but it is likely that their use is rather extensive. Certainly some kind of evaluation system is being used to determine promotions, grant or deny tenure, and determine salary adjustments. In fact, most colleges and universities now openly admit that salary improvements are made on the basis of merit (necessarily requiring some system for judging effectiveness, formal or otherwise). This method replaces a system of "across the board" raises based on level of preparation and extent of experience.

An examination of the literature describing the evaluative processes now in use reveals a wide diversity of types and procedures. Rating instruments in greatest use contain assessment items which fall into three basic categories: (1) personal qualities (the kind of person an organization prefers to employ, to retain, and to reward); (2) professional qualities, such as "is aware of recent developments in his field"; and (3) teaching performance—descriptions of specific practices and behaviors desired by the employing system. Some instruments require that the person being evaluated describe activities currently underway, those recently completed, and those contemplated to further the individual's professional growth.

But widespread variations are noted when one examines the literature describing the manner with which evaluation instruments are developed and how they are operated. Some instruments are developed unilaterally by administrators and are completed in a similarly arbitrary—and unwise—way. Other instruments are the products of committees of teachers who will be later evaluated by these instruments. While some instruments are completed only by administrators, other systems include provisions for judgments to be made by the person being evaluated, by his peers (especially important at the university level), increasingly by students, and occasionally by parents.

No universally accepted or widely applicable instrument, or evaluation system, exists. This should not be surprising, considering the state of the art. Nor is it necessarily bad, for a good case can be made for an organization's devising its own plan, one that seems most applicable, acceptable, and workable in a specific situation. But it is not necessary for each organization to "re-invent the wheel." Many tested instruments and procedures in use now should be studied by managers who are devising their own systems, or modifying an existing one. These managers might profit from a review of the report from Educational Research Service, cited earlier, which contains samples of several procedures and instruments now in operation, along with an overall report on the extent and nature of teacher evaluation throughout the country. The educational manager concerned with performance evaluation of administrative and other support personnel may find the companion report helpful.

At the university level, *Evaluating Faculty Performance*, by Richard I. Miller[12] examines several assumptions about faculty evaluation, some illustrative appraisal forms, and various components of the professor's overall work which should be included. Of help also might be Report 13 of *ERIC Clearinghouse on Higher Education*.[13] This report, after addressing itself to the problems associated with the measurement of teaching performance and describing some approaches currently being used in colleges and universities, describes one model by which teacher effectiveness might be evaluated.

Assistance in viewing teacher behavior in the evaluation process may be gained from a publication by Allen, Barnes, Reece and Roberson entitled *Teacher Self-Appraisal: A Way of Looking Over Your Own Shoulder*.[14] These authors discuss various ways by which teaching behavior can be viewed externally and then describe ways teachers can engage in self-appraisal. They also point out several hazards which may be involved in the latter approach.

In addition, the authors offer the following suggestions for those educational managers who are establishing performance evaluation programs. With appropriate modification, these suggestions may also be used as criteria for evaluating existing programs.

Performance evaluation systems should:

1. Be based on a rational, well-thought-out concept of performance effectiveness rather than an assortment of truisms and conventional wisdoms.

2. Have a good research base: that is, utilize those findings from research conducted locally and elsewhere which describe the values certain performances have over others.

3. Include in their development all groups and agencies who will be significantly involved in both the outcomes of the process and the responsibility for making decisions which are related to such findings (tenure, promotion, salary, assignment).

4. Emphasize "measurable" expectations as opposed to nebulous cliches. For example, the expectation that a teacher will make "daily instructional plans" lends itself to measurement much more realistically than does the expectation that he will "maintain a good classroom atmosphere."

5. Emphasize those performances which research has indicated correlate closely with effective performance as opposed to vague, unproven generalities. For example, if an organization values the questioning-technique whereby a teacher is expected to move students from the level of memory to evaluation, observations can be made by competent persons to determine a teacher's skill in this regard with much more certainty than by observing his "classroom atmosphere."

6. Reflect, philosophically and operationally, that evaluation is a continuous process. Many currently used systems require only "one shot" evaluation, such as at the end of a probationary period when a teacher is being considered for tenure, or each spring when salary adjustments and promotions are being considered at the college level.

7. Avoid the obvious but nonetheless frequently found pitfalls which sabotage the effective implementation of otherwise sound programs.

(a.) The person being evaluated has little or no involvement in the process.

(b.) Those who conduct the evaluation often are not in position to perform the evaluation and are not competent to do so. The most frequent objection given by classroom teachers to the idea of performance evaluation (especially when it is linked with some plan of merit pay) is

that principals (or corresponding administrators in higher education) are not capable, by virtue of preparation or experience, to make accurate evaluative judgments about their teaching. Instructional supervisors typically are better qualified for this task and often are more acceptable to teachers. But supervisory personnel often do not have the authority base necessary to have their observation and judgments appropriately considered and acted upon.

(c.) Persons who often are in the best position to evaluate (peers and students) typically are omitted from the evaluation process. The contention is made increasingly that some aspects of competency (such as depth and currency of knowledge in one's teaching field) can be judged most accurately only by one's peers. This is heard quite frequently now in higher education but is probably true in grades K-12 also. By the same token, student opinion and judgments are rarely used in the formal evaluation of education, resulting not only in the system having a reduced information base but also forcing students to devise their own system (usually even less acceptable to teachers) for evaluating teachers and administrators. "Informal" systems being developed by students today go far beyond the "scouting" system long ago developed by sororities and fraternities. Increased militancy of students and improved means of processing and disseminating information have resulted in teacher and course evaluation systems being rather common on college campuses and increasingly within secondary schools. Such efforts toward evaluation are not viewed here as being undesirable, but rather as being less effective than student involvement legitimized from the outset, and better use of such involvement. It is no easy task, however, to interpret student opinions. expectations and appraisals, or to relate them to the philosophy involving a particular system of evaluation.

In summary, much progress has been made in the field of performance evaluation. Most of the action has been in regard to evaluating teaching, but more and more all personnel are coming under the umbrella of performance evaluation. The educator who longs for the day when his profession will be characterized by a viable system for "self policing" may be encouraged by the fact that today about 90% of all public schools, and perhaps a higher percentage of colleges and universities, have formalized systems of performance evaluation. There is a sufficient array of instruments and procedures available now to provide the creative and aggressive educational manager with good resources with which to work in this important area of responsibility

Let us look now at the third basic way performance can be evaluated, although at the moment it is probably less well perfected than the system we have just discussed.

Evaluation By Measuring Output of Efforts

Many educators look wistfully to the day when it is possible (if indeed it ever will be) to conduct evaluations in terms of a one-to-one, direct relationship between process and outcome. They long for a simplistic way of being able to say, for example, that a particular behavior by a teacher caused a particular behavior to result in the learner—a cause-and-effect relationship. Many laymen, including some politicians, think this day has already arrived and go about routinely expressing evaluative judgments as if this were true.

Arguments about how near we are to a cause-and-effect way of evaluating are rather premature at this point of time, as argued by Eric L. Lindman:

> To regard an 18-year-old youth in the graduating class as a product* of his high school implies more responsibility than the school can accept. His behavior is influenced by many factors beyond the control of his school. The time-honored allies of the school in the child-rearing process—the church, the YMCA, the Boy Scouts, the Camp Fire Girls—are still with us, but they are losing their effectiveness. So is Horatio Alger's message to youth that hard work and dedication bring success.

---

*Lindman uses the term "product" within the context of the drive toward accountability, a more recent and widely used substitute for the cause-and-effect relationship.

> Along with the deterioration of these familiar guideposts is
> the triumphal entry of television. The new Pied Piper is
> preempting more and more of the waking hours of children
> and youth, providing a powerful distraction from the
> school's three R's, which have low Neilson Ratings.
> Unfortunately, this twentieth century Pied Piper spends a
> disproportionate amount of time selling soap and cereals.[15]

Even the profession of medicine (which many feel is the most
highly developed of all professions) has not advanced to the point
that the recipient of services rendered is charged *only* if the
intended results accrue; however, legal fees are sometimes less
if the verdict goes against the client. Rather, all professions,
including education, typically operate on the basis of the degree
to which practices followed in rendering the service are congruent
with what the profession has approved.

It seems fair to say that performance evaluation in education is
much like it is in other professions in that the process rather than
the product is the usual basis for reaching evaluative judgments.
The continuum of Campbell and others (discussed earlier)
illustrated that evaluation is more difficult in those activities
involving human interaction and outcomes and where the
intended result is in the intangible realm of attitudes as opposed
to products—for example, a minister or a psychiatrist trying
to help a person achieve inner peace as contrasted with a fac-
tory worker producing ping pong balls.

Why, then, in the face of these constraints and obstacles do we
cite this as one way of evaluating performance? The answer is that
for the artistic (and courageous) educational manager there is
much to be gained from the use of this approach. Consider several
examples of actual events in education in which performance
evaluation was achieved quite effectively. Remember that the
essence of our theme here is the relationship between effort
(purpose and practice) and outcome (product).

A football coach has as one of his purposes the winning of ball
games. It is hoped, of course, that other purposes are involved
too, such as character development, improvement of human
relationships, and physical development. But one of the reasons
team contests are played is to see which team is better on a
particular occasion.

One coach known by the authors amassed near-perfect records in diverse school settings. He became known as a winner, a person who could quickly turn a losing situation into a winning one, including winning attitudes as well as winning records.

But, it could be charged that he used educationally unsound tactics and procedures that prevented the achievement of other and perhaps more important objectives. Such was not the case. In fact, those persons close to the situation contended that the achievement of related goals and objectives was even more spectacular. School spirit surged in each instance and remains high today. Upon visits back home, former players regularly called on him to express appreciation for what he had meant to them and often to seek his advice and counsel. Some named their sons after him. The city named the stadium in his honor. The school principal relied on him to help counsel students with serious problems.

Most readers can recall similar examples of outstanding performance. Perhaps it was a music teacher who consistently produced "winning teams" without using undesirable practices and means; a science teacher whose students year after year won record numbers of science fair awards; or the English teacher whose students always excelled in college English courses. Or was it a college dean who on more than one occasion dramatically renovated programs, instilled "winning ways" and attitudes in faculty and students wherever he went? Or maybe it was a vice president for student affairs who helped students find their place within the college community and become constructive learners rather than disgruntled dissidents.

The point here is that by looking deep and carefully, with a keen understanding of the purpose-practice-outcome relationship, the artistic educational manager can utilize the technique of evaluating on the basis of outcomes—or the lack of them. Two precautions are in order, however.

First, the temptation is great to reward for instant success, before it is possible to ascertain that a success pattern exists and that undesirable side effects do not accompany the desired outcomes. Violations of this principle are found in and out of education. Some college officials have named buildings for persons who have done much for the institutions only to find out a few years later that those persons must go to prison for the misuse of public funds.

Second, it is difficult, at times impossible, to know how much of the success can be attributed to a particular person. The college dean who seemed to make major improvements single-handedly may have been greatly aided by the simultaneous commitment by the university (which received little publicity) to overhaul that program area, resulting in strong moral and fiscal support in the form of increased positions, salary adjustments, and so forth. Without analysis, it would be easy to conclude that these improvements were achievements of the dean, rather than support factors not highly publicized.

In any event, two suggestions for the educational manager seem warranted in terms of his use of this approach to performance evaluation. First, he should not resist the occasional and artistic use of the process of evaluation on the basis of outcome. But he should use it delicately, with keen awareness of its limitations and potential for misuse, and with caution and wisdom. Second, he should be alert to the fact that not only laymen but professionals as well have a natural tendency to rely unduly on this technique and to misuse it frequently. He may find himself in the frustrating position of finding it necessary to dismiss a first-year coach who won all his games but who had misrepresented himself in the employment process and who had several serious educational deficiencies less visible to the community than his 10-0 winning record.

Whereas evaluation in terms of output is still extremely difficult when the desired output involves human behavior, recent achievements in the field of management by objectives make the process less difficult and hold great potential for use in evaluation where objectives are concerned with output not necessarily humanistic in nature. Readers interested in exploring the potential of management by objectives in the process of evaluation may find the book by George S. Odiorne, *Management By Objectives*, to be a helpful resource.[16]

Summary

Probably no area of educational management places more stress on the incumbent than does the matter of performance evaluation. To achieve it effectively is difficult, fraught with controversy and danger, and usually low on the scale for receiving accolades and awards. To default leads to chaos and educational anarchy.

Several factors penalize the educational manager in his efforts to develop and operate an effective program of performance evaluation. Chief among these are the intangibility and latency of educational outcomes; the troublesome lack of consensus regarding purposes and goals; the historic resistance to evaluation by teacher groups and organizations; the varied and sundry jobs which the teacher is expected to perform in addition to the primary one—teaching; and the low state of the art in regard to a solid understanding of the cause-effect relationship.

These obstacles and barriers notwithstanding, the educational manager no longer has an option between seeing that a program for evaluating performance is operated or choosing not to do so. He can find encouragement, and assistance, from several recent developments. The more salient of these developments are (1) the increased involvement and power granted educators; (2) great strides made in educators' ability and willingness to state goals and objectives behaviorally and in measurable terms; and (3) a series of new teaching-learning constructs and strategies. Each of these developments moves us closer to the day when performance in education can be evaluated with sufficient confidence and competence to raise it to real professional status.

At present there are three basic approaches to performance evaluation. Although the first of these is really "before the fact," it does allow employing administrators and governing boards to select those persons who have completed preparation programs which best meet the employers' expectations and whose previous experience has been judged to be competent by people whom the employers respect.

The second basic approach is still rather new. Only recently have the vast majority of educational institutions developed systems whereby value judgments are made regarding characteristics, qualities, and performance, and upon which evaluative judgements relative to the degree of congruency between expectations and performance, are subsequently made. Much benefit is believed to be accruing to the education profession and to students as a result of the recent and widespread use of this system of performance evaluation. But this system leaves us short of the one seemingly most highly desired by educators and laymen alike; that is, evaluation on the basis of outcome.

The system of evaluating in terms of outcome is not fully developed in any professional field, and perhaps is developed less well in education than in other professions: A case was presented, however, for utilizing the system in certain ways and under certain conditions.

Perhaps no other area of the total responsibilities usually assigned to the educational manager calls for more courage, more acumen, and more wisdom to accompany the knowledge base than the area of performance evaluation. Knowing what should be done by way of evaluation, exercising the wisdom needed, and mustering the courage to act upon findings and conclusions are truly acts of artistic educational management.

DISCUSSION QUESTIONS/LEARNING ACTIVITIES

1. To what extent are the barriers to performance evaluation described in this chapter fundamentally attributable to a lack of administrative responsibility and courage?

2. Educational managers have frequently been accused of being non-innovative and tradition-bound. Identify which of the "promising practices" described by the authors (and others which you might wish to add) were initiated or promoted by educational managers.

3. Do faculties lack a sufficient information base to evaluate managerial performance? Should educational managers be evaluated by multiple groups—faculty, governing boards, students? Give reasons for your answer.

4. Develop a rating scale for the evaluation of an educational management position such as college dean or school principal. Determine to what extent the rating scale portrays a concept of role and responsibility. Administer the scale to selected persons who might evaluate the position you have in mind.

5. What position have major teacher-oriented educational organizations (such as NEA, AFT, AAUP) taken on the question of performance evaluation? Conduct a search of appropriate literature or interview leaders in these organizations to provide data on this question. How do you assess their positions? What are the implications for educational management?

6. Arrange for a debate on the issue of performance evaluation. Resolved: Evaluation of Teaching Performance by One's Peers is Superior to That Conducted by Appropriate Educational Managers.

NOTES

1. Roald F. Campbell, Edwin M. Bridges, John E. Corbally, Jr., Raphael O. Nystrand, John A. Ramseyer, *Introduction to Educational Administration,* 4th edition (Boston: Allyn & Bacon, 1971), p. 130.

2. James L. Olivero, *Micro-Teaching: Medium For Improving Instruction,* Foundation of Education Services (Columbus, O.: Charles E. Merrill, 1970), p. 31.

3. Benjamin S. Bloom (ed.), *Taxonomy of Educational Objectives* (New York: Longmons, Green, 1956).

4. Robert J. Armstrong, Terry Q. Cornell, Robert E. Kramer, and E. Wayne Roberson, *The Development and Evaluation of Behavioral Objectives* (Worthington, O.: Charles A. Jones, 1970), pp. 55-82.

5. Robert F. Mager, *Preparing Instructional Objectives* (Palo Alto, Calif.: Fearon, 1962), p. v.

6. Norris M. Sanders, *Classroom Questions: What Kinds* (New York: Harper & Row, 1966).

7. Leon M. Lessinger, "Accountability to Public Education," *Journal of the National Education Association,* Vol. 59, No. 5, May 1970, p. 52.

8. Herbert I. Von Haden and Jean Marie King, *Educational Innovator's Guide* (Worthington, O.: Charles A. Jones, 1974), p. 441.

9. Kenneth Cadenhead and Laura Newell, "Personalizing Teacher Education," *Educational Technology,* March 1973, p. 51.

10. "Evaluating Teaching Performance," *Educational Research Service,* Circular No. 2 (Washington D.C.: Educational Research Service, 1972), p. 1.

11. "Evaluating Administrative/Supervisory Performance," *Educational Research Service,* Circular No. 6, (Washington D. C.: Educational Research Service, 1972).

12. Richard I. Miller, *Evaluating Faculty Performance* (London: Jossey Bass, 1972).

13. Marvin J. Cook and Richard F. Neville, "The Faculty as Teachers: A Perspective on Evaluation," Report 13, *ERIC Clearinghouse on Higher Education* (Washington D. C.: George Washington University, September, 1971).

14. Paul M. Allen, William D. Barnes, Jerald L. Reece, and E. Wayne Roberson, *Teacher Self-Appraisal: A Way of Looking Over Your Own Shoulder* (Worthington, O.: Charles A. Jones, 1970).

15. Eric L. Lindman, "The Means and Ends of Accountability," Proceedings of the Conference on Educational Accountability, sponsored by Educational Testing Service, Chicago, Illinois, June, 1971 (Princeton: Educational Testing Service, 1971), p. B-4.

16. George S. Odiorne, *Management By Objectives* (New York: Pitman, 1965).

12
Improving Educational Leadership

> *Men who boast of being what is called "practical"*
> *are for the most part exclusively preoccupied with*
> *means. But theirs is only one-half of wisdom. When*
> *we take account of the other half, which is concerned*
> *with ends, the economic process and the whole of*
> *human life take on an entirely new aspect. We ask no*
> *longer: What have the producers produced, and what*
> *has consumption enabled the consumers in their turn*
> *to produce? We ask instead: What has there been in*
> *the lives of the consumers and producers to make them*
> *glad to be alive?*
>
> Bertrand Russell, *Authority and the Individual*

A common charge in education today is that too many educational managers are losing their capacity for leadership. They have become prisoners of their organizations—slaves to process, captured by their calendars, commanded by committees, intimidated by structure, inundated by information, tyrannized by trivia. The infrequency of significant personal leadership, it is argued, accounts for the relatively simple organizational geometry of some schools and colleges. They tend to move in straight lines, getting bigger but not necessarily better. And now some school systems and colleges do not even enjoy the conventional benchmark of progress—growth.

What are the factors that inhibit educational leadership? There are no simple answers. Perhaps one of the reasons is that too often performance is not anchored in knowledge. One can identify at least a few superintendents, college deans, elementary principals, and college presidents whose preparation for the challenges they face is shallow indeed.

These are not times for management amateurs in education. Amateurs know nothing of management concepts, and often believe that it is not necessary to know. Neither is this a time for

management robots—those who are slaves to PERT charts, program budgeting systems, and MBO systems. Rather, it is a time for educational managers who recognize the practical promise of ideas, who realize that without knowledge they will be buffeted about by every force large or small. We are managers of an array of resources—physical, technological, financial—and the most precious of them all—human resources. We are called upon to manage these in an environment that demands both personal and social sensitivity. Superintendent or supervisor, dean or director, president or provost— effective performance is improbable unless it is based on understanding and application of the knowledge of our field.

However, a colleague whose knowledge foundation is restricted is not the greatest tragedy of our profession today. The great professional sadness today should be for those educational managers who are masters of process but ignorant of purpose. Preoccupied with means but insensitive to ends, their achievement is devoid of meaning. Their philosophy permits them to value only those things that have utility. They know and apply management concepts from a technical perspective but fail to sense that the most precious dimension of education lies in the bonded fellowship between student and teacher, and in the world of ideas that unites them in common dedication to learning.

However, if we are masters of process but oblivious to purpose, if we are enamored of means but insensitive to ends, then we have only "one half of wisdom." The other half of wisdom lies in the ends we seek and the values we hold. If we fail in our leadership obligations, it may be because we have substituted means for ends. It may be because we are diverted from our purposes. An exploration of these dimensions of our obligations may prove helpful in uncovering ways for increasing leadership effectiveness.

The Record of Our Emptiness -
A Substitution of Means for Ends

Today's educational manager is caught in a web of forces that constrain his best efforts, frustrate his best intentions, and confound his best plans. Some of these forces originate within; they result in a substitution of means for ends. And some originate without; they produce a distraction from purpose.

In schools and colleges there is a tendency to focus energy and attention more on process (teaching) than on purpose (learning). A similar substitution of means for ends plagues some educational managers. The substitution diminishes true effectiveness. Here are a few of the more common means that have become ends—processes masquerading as purpose.

Growth

Most educational managers have internalized a set of benchmarks by which they measure progress and performance. What are some of these?

For some, the performance ends are growth. For them, the measures of achievement are visible, concrete, easy-to-measure. They are to be found in increased operating budgets, increased replacement value of the physical plant, increased faculty numbers and student enrollments. These are tangible and public indicators. They make attractive and impressive graphs for annual reports. The question is not whether they are essential indicators of managerial performance, but rather whether these should be the only measures. Growth is not always progress, nor is growth always good. Too late are we finding out that extraordinarily large institutions may be wasteful of dollars and talent that could be better spent in institutions of less massive configurations.

Some of us write bold lines but on perishable bond. We keep company with landscape architects, computer marketing specialists, systems engineers, management consultants, building contractors, and government officials. Necessary company, but not sufficient; for it is not this company that feels the frustration of an incompetent teacher or the anxiety of working for a division director with a "Simon Legree" style. Thus, those educational managers whose concept of acceptable performance can be found only in a growth chart with a positive slope need to rethink their priorities.

Mobility

Is the mark of managerial accomplishment to be found in the speed with which we climbed the executive ladder? Has the world noted, and does it really care, that we were first a director and then a dean, first a teacher and then a principal, first a supervisor and then a superintendent? For some educational managers, the marks of mobility are an appropriate and legitimate testimony to their talent and energy. For others, a mania for upper mobility blinds them to the need for a job well executed where they serve.

A young doctoral graduate had high aspirations and ambitions. In his first position as executive assistant to the president of a large university, he became infatuated by the power and prestige associated with that office and began to sacrifice career content for career status. He moved in all the correct social ways but never knew what it was like down in the engine room of the university, never knew what it was like to get dirty in dealing with all the machinery of a large organization, never knew the frustrations of dealing with the bureaucracy. What he wanted he did not realize. He severely curtailed a promising career because he mistook the facade for the substance of educational leadership.

Educational managers who see mobility as an end have failed to discern that there is no royal road to an effective match of talent and task. Each is tailor-made. There are college presidents who are Rhodes scholars and an occasional president, equally effective, who may not be sure what a Rhodes scholar is. There are school superintendents who were teachers and an occasional superintendent, equally effective, who did not teach. There are deans who are poets and an occasional dean, equally effective, who thinks that Socrates played second base for the Cubs. There are principals who were coaches and an occasional principal, equally effective, who was a band director.

A small town principal in a Southern state gave 30 years of his life to a single high school. By most measures of performance he was not very successful. He did not become a supervisor or superintendent. Yet the record of his achievement is written out in the lives of men and women for whom he cared. He cared by providing the best faculty. He cared by providing a model of personal and professional integrity in school and community. He cared by displaying an artistic mix of discipline and nurture.

Upward mobility is not an infallible measure of achievement, not a satisfactory end to be sought. A complete incompetent can survive in most of our schools and colleges for a minimum of three years—the higher the position, the easier the survival—one year to learn the ropes and enjoy the honeymoon accorded the new man, a second year for students, faculty, and colleagues to discover the incompetence, and a third or a fourth year for colleagues to find a humanistic way of solving the problem. Thus, some managers, having discovered this "secret" never exhibit enough staying power for anyone to discover whether they have any substance.

Properly viewed, mobility to more responsible positions should reflect service rendered to our students, faculties, colleagues—and not an end in itself.

Involvement

Another means which displaces ends in the record of some educational managers is that of involvement. The measure of effective performance becomes a quantitative affair which is measured in the length of one's vita and the list of civic and professional organizations to which he belongs. The *sine qua non* of the effective manager is related not to achievement but to visibility. The proper application of social intelligence is essential for effective management, but when that application produces token activity in civic, church, and professional activities—activity rooted in convention rather than conviction —then the substitution of means for ends is too obvious to ignore.

The new academic dean of a metropolitan community college enjoyed music. Singing with the community chorale would have been an artistic, even therapeutic, outlet for his talent. His president, however, was of a different persuasion, anxious to make the proper appearances. The energy and spirit of the dean were soon drained away in an endless set of conventions, the weekly meetings of two civic clubs and countless other "appearances." Neither the community nor the college profited from this shotgun pattern of energy expenditure.

Significant and extraordinary in intensity, the social expectations for educational managers should not be ignored. For in the eyes of many, where we are found—and with whom—is an expression of our interest, our concern. And where we are not found is an expression of our apathy.

But what of these expectations? If we do not attend every football game, does this mean that we do not value the importance of sports? If we do not personally examine the bandroom at the new high school, does this mean that we do not value music? If we do not attend Rotary every week, does this mean that we do not care for community? If we do not greet the opening of the Shakespeare festival on our campus, does this mean that we do not care for literature and the labors of our English and drama faculty? If we do not attend the opening of the student festival, does this mean that we are not interested in our students?

Is it possible for the educational manager to avoid the torture rack of competing interests, to avoid becoming the prisoner of the expectations of others? Attempting to respond to every interest not only saps our energy but reinforces the notion that managers are supposed to do so. There are solutions described later in this chapter, that permit us to use involvement wisely rather than as an end itself.

Activity

For some educational managers, activity rather than achievement becomes the end. The assumption seems to be that if they are busy, then they are effective. The form this substitution can take is of infinite variety. For example, some managers make a great show of the hours they work. They arrive early, stay late, work over weekends—but make sure that all about them know this. And unfortunately, they frequently impress their style upon those with whom they work.

Those in the organization somewhat removed see this as a noble gesture, undertaken at great personal sacrifice. They feed these educational managers a host of verbal reinforcers which only imbeds the pattern more deeply. Now there's nothing inherently wrong with a professional truly dedicated to his job nor anything out of the ordinary about long hours. Indeed, most managers find it absolutely essential to find a few quiet moments before or after regular hours in which to catch up on the reflective dimensions of their jobs, to deal with those planning and evaluation matters that cannot be handled with crowded calendars during the regular day.

But it is professionally pathetic to see an educational manager making a great show out of long hours when he fritters away regular hours in gossip, disorganization, or other dysfunctional activity which is a product of his management incompetence.

Another manifestation of this activity syndrome is the manager who keeps his organization in constant turmoil and conflict. He has the notion that challenge, tension, and threat are essential to organizational and personal health. Properly managed, these can be. But when conflict and tension are deliberately provoked so that the manager can satisfy his own ego in reducing that conflict, or when conflict and tension are not balanced by stability and security, then we must ask questions about the relationship of ends and means.

A college dean spent 15 years in the same position. He was not upwardly mobile. He did not become vice president nor president. He was modestly active in church and community. He arrived at work most mornings at 8:00 or 8:30 and left most afternoons by 5:00. On special occasions, such as registration, he could be found at work after hours. And on Saturday mornings he took coffee with students and friends.

During the time he was at work, the careful discipline of his time, a trusting investment in a good staff, the force of his commitment, and the authority of his personality inspired qualitative program improvements throughout his college. He was near to the concerns of students, patient with the troubled, and summary in his treatment of the arrogant. The quality of his judgment and caring was clear to all. He was confidant to clerk typists, students, faculty, administrator colleagues, and the president of the institution.

The strength of his conviction was tested by more than one opponent, and his honesty refreshingly different. He could make artistic and effective application of tension and conflict because they occurred in relationships that were nurtured and prepared by stability and security. A quiet professional whose leadership was not to be measured in terms of growth, not in his own mobility, not in the record of his involvements, and not in a rush of activity, but in the ideals he engendered in the lives of students and colleagues. When he retired from the university, the accounts receivable carried no record of his contribution; but the affection carried in the hearts of those who knew him revealed that he possessed the complete wisdom of the true managerial artist.

The Record of our Distractions - A Challenge to Purposeful Effort

Losing sight of the enduring purposes of our role, substituting means for ends, focusing on process rather than purpose, we diminish the force of our leadership. If this hazard of managerial life were not enough, there is also present in our daily environment a set of external forces that act to distract us further. Complications crowd into our calendar and present us with a multiplicity of demands that lead not to unity of effort but to fragmentation. To remain goal-centered in the midst of these distractions is difficult.

Tyrannized by Trivia

Because they are at the top of some part or all of the organizational pyramid, educational managers are constantly sought out by a variety of peoples. Appointment calendars are filled with matters of varying degrees of importance. The natural inclination of most managers is to be accessible, but our energy and our initiative can be drained away by an inordinate reverence for routine.

Writing in the *Saturday Review*, Warren Bennis, a management and organization scholar and president of the University of Cincinnati, tells what faced him as he took over the presidency there:

> Here's a note from a professor, complaining that his
> classroom temperature is down to 65. I suppose that he
> expects me to grab a wrench and fix it. A student complains
> that we won't give him credit for acting as assistant to a city
> councilman. Another was unable to get into the student
> health center. The teacher at my child's day school, who is
> also a student at U of C, is dissatisfied with her grades. A
> parent complains about the four letter words in a Philip
> Roth book being used in an English class. The track coach
> wants me to come over to see for myself how bad the track is.
> An alumnus couldn't get the football seat he wanted.
> Another wants the coach fired. A teacher just called to tell
> me the squash court was closed at 7:00 p.m. when he wanted
> to use it.[1]

Bennis goes on to point out that this tyranny of trivia, if
unchecked, could keep him from spending any reflective time on
the direction and goals of the university.

Loss of Solitude

A cluttered calendar and a busy telephone divert us from
spending any significant energy and attention on the goals of our
organization or activity. Many educational managers find that
once the day is under way, they move to the pleasure of others, a
slave to events. But Eugene E. Jennings asks us to consider who
may be most responsible for this state of affairs:

> . . . this annihilation of privacy is to some extent
> self-inflicted. The typical executive fears isolation, dreads
> what will happen if he is alone with himself. He welcomes
> intrusion into his privacy and is only too happy to go to
> meetings and be with people . . . The tragedy in not
> having the necessary will power to resist the present social
> trend is that the annihilation of privacy leads to the
> annihilation of the person or self.[2]

In our busy pursuit of the centrifugal activities of our schools
and colleges, we have forgotten the advantages of and the
necessity for being alone. We remain strangers to ourselves and
fail to replenish those personal resources that are depleted each

day. Drained of the intellectual and emotional potential essential to leadership, we can do no other than become the slave to events about us.

Too few educational managers practice the art of aloneness. But it is not surprising; for it is an interesting and perhaps sad commentary on our social milieu that being alone is often considered suspect. Some managers find the will to row against this current because they have discovered the power of self-renewal that comes from moments alone.

A large university president regularly spent one month each summer away from his institution, resting and reflecting in a hideaway cabin deep in a Western wood. While some presidents believe that their institutions would fall to pieces during their extended absence, this president had more impact on the direction of his institution as a result of his time spent apart—time in which he could reflect not only on goals of his institution but on the patterns of organization and personnel required to meet these goals.

Inundated with Information

Another factor that distracts us from the goals of our schools and colleges is a flood of information. One academic manager characterized the information overflow as "huge piles of IBM feces."[3] Thus, the disarray of memos, reports, and greenbar computer paper on our desks is a testimony to a lack of artistry in information management.

Information is an important and powerful resource. Unfortunately, information is more frequently an impediment rather than a resource. Too many educational organizations are burdened with information idiots who do not know what staff work is. They pile the vice president's or deputy superintendent's desk high with reams of paper rather than giving him a crisp and concise staff report, with incisive analysis, clear decision alternatives, and a recommendation for action.

At the other end of the continuum, we have those information wizards who make endless information demands without giving sufficient attention to how the information will be applied nor to the processes required to translate raw data into meaningful information. What is missing is that sense of managerial artistry that reminds us that information should be obtained not because it would be nice to have but because, with it, decisions can be made with greater wisdom.

Oppressed by Structure and Process

Educational institutions are not organized to receive new ideas. The myriad points of review and deliberation which appear essential to the approval of any new ideas can constitute an oppression of structure and process.

If you have an idea about policy or program, you must consider the agony required to push this idea through the standing committees and deliberative councils. Ideas that go into our decision systems in education, clean and direct, can come out complicated and distorted after all vested interest groups have added their amendments.

The Record of our Disobedience -
A Renaissance of Personal Sovereignty

In the face of the impeding forces and other pressures, some educational managers are finding faculty life more attractive, and some have run away to other pursuits. And some are taking the path marked by Clark Kerr who was writing about higher education managers when he said:

> Many administrators today are concentrating on a low profile and personal survival. The times, however, require a more active approach to guide constructive change and to resolve conflicts in productive ways.[4]

In the decade of the 1960s, some educational managers— presidents and principals, deans and directors—were little more than educational midwives, helping institutions move along in directions they would have moved anyway. This is not a style that most of us will have the liberty to enjoy in the years to come. If we are interested in bringing about a renaissance of

personal sovereignty in our schools and colleges, then we must be disobedient to some of the forces we have outlined.

It is a time for heroic and conspicuous personalities, for educational managers who recognize the leadership obligations of their role and move to give that leadership. Few, if any, graduate courses are now offered on the suggestions below, but these reflections may contain keys that will open the lock to more purposeful performance.

A Sense of Mission

If we are to overcome the distractions mentioned earlier, we must be able to define what is important. History teaches us that there are few forces more powerful than those resident in that man or woman who has a deep and disturbing sense of mission. The necessity for defining what is important is clearly outlined in a paper by Arthur Combs entitled "The Human Aspect of Administration." He suggested that:

> "What you think is important" sounds like a very simple idea, but it turns out to be absolutely basic to the whole question of what makes a person an effective helper. Applied to the field of administration, this is perhaps the most outstanding single reason for the failure of administrators to carry out their job, the failure to clarify in their own minds what is really important. What happens is that they get on a kind of merry-go-round in which because they don't know what is important, everything is important. When everything is important you have to do everything. The people see you doing everything and they expect you to do everything and that keeps you so busy that you don't have time to think about what is important.[5]

The history of great accomplishment is written by men and women with a sense of mission who insist on doing those things others tell them are impossible.

A Sense of Wonder

A second and simple factor essential to the exercise of leadership is curiosity or what we might call a sense of wonder. A piece of verse from a book by James Kavanaugh* entitled "I Wonder," goes like this:

> I wonder if the waves get weary
> > With the surf and surfers on their backs
> Or if the wind is angry when
> > It throws the rain against my window
> I wonder if the mountains are lonely
> > Or only sad
> I wonder if the gulls are sick of eating fish
> > If the sandpipers get tired of dodging waves?
> Maybe we could send a man from earth
> > To study the stress on the waves
> > To chart the temper of the wind
> > And the temperature of the mountains
> > To tell the desert jokes until the sage shakes with laughter
> > To feed the gulls a balanced diet with mineral supplements
> > And the sandpipers? We'll tune them into TV
> > To hear the future of the tides.
>
> I wonder funny things—like: Do sandcrabs live in condominiums?

Is this a silly verse? Not at all. Some of the most auspicious moments in the history of ideas have come from moments of play, from moments of free-floating curiosity. The record of human progress is a chronicle of individuals who continually ask the simple question "why?"

A Sense of Adventure

The exercise of managerial leadership in our schools and colleges requires a sense of adventure, a willingness to emerge from the anonymity of our organizations and offices, to recognize that few worthwhile marks in the history of human endeavor take place without personal risk, to grow and develop in struggle with challenge.

---

*Copyright© 1971 by James Kavanaugh. From the book *Will You Be My Friend?* by James Kavanaugh. Reprinted by permission of Nash Publishing Corp., Los Angeles.

Many of us run in fear of mistakes. Are we laboring on the assumption that we are potentially perfect? A mistake is at least a declaration of our humanness. Or are we insecure in our personal professional identity? A strong sense of identity is not constructed out of fear and no-risk involvements.

A Sense of Discipline

Effective leadership requires a discipline of our personal resources, the most important of which may be our time. Drucker says:

> [The] effective executive knows that time is the limiting factor. The output limits of any process are set by the scarcest resource. In the process we call "accomplishment," this is time.[6]

A quick diagnosis of our time distribution will probably reveal that time is wasted because of one or more of these factors:

1. A system of policy and procedures that produces recurring crisis.
2. An organizational pattern in which too many people are reporting to the executive.
3. A managerial style in which the executive holds all decision reins in his hands—the effect of which is to limit the power of his staff to act and forces more people to him directly as the principal source of decision power.

A sense of discipline will also assist us in consolidating time into sizable blocks essential for concentrated work on a single problem. Depending on the size of the problem, this may mean two hours held out of the appointment calendar each morning, three or four weeks in retreat, getting to the office an hour before everyone else, or remaining in the quiet of the evening. The discipline required is to find and protect that block of time. Finally, a sense of discipline will enable us to seize one major problem or challenge at a time and dispatch it rather than fragmenting our effort all over the organizational landscape.

A Sense of Personal Concern

What is needed is leadership. But what we are expected to give we should also cultivate in colleagues. A neglected role of the educational manager is that of teaching. The selection and placement of aspiring educational managers does not end our responsibility. That responsibility includes more than finding a position and a challenge. It includes an element of nurture, of guidance, of developmental attention—delivered with the same concern and requiring the same personal investment as that found in any dedicated and effective teacher.

But we will have to realize as well that potential leaders do not always make agreeable subordinates. They may appear insolent, egocentric, argumentative, conceited, arrogant, critical. Potential leaders may also have high confidence in their own judgment. While this is an essential characteristic for those who inspire others to action, it is not a quality that superiors always find endearing. The ability to work with and cultivate this kind of potential is a mark of managerial strength and courage.

A Concluding Note

This is our theme. Educational managers are in danger of abdicating their leadership obligations. Too often we have substituted means for ends, focusing our attention on process rather than purpose. We have equated growth, mobility, involvement, and activity with performance and progress. We have permitted ourselves to be diverted from the goals of our organization. Our privacy is taken by committees and conferences. We are tyrannized by trivia and inundated with information. Our energy is drained away in dealing with the oppression of overly complicated decision structures and processes.

Our plea is for educational managers whose performance is disobedient to these forces. It is for men and women who will be successful managers of change and conflict because their performance is anchored in knowledge. It is for educational leaders who are conspicuous in personality, who, in the words of Thoreau, hear a different drummer and have the courage to step to the music they hear. It is for colleagues whose sense of mission, curiosity, adventure, discipline and care persuades us to abandon comfortable positions from which we can know neither adventure nor failure. It is for professionals who understand that schools and colleges do not exist to be managed, that they exist for ideas and learning. It is for educators who understand that accomplishment in the life of learning, as in any other dimension of human endeavor, requires leadership, and who move with sensitivity of purpose and process to give that leadership.

DISCUSSION QUESTIONS/LEARNING ACTIVITIES

1. In this chapter, we have identified some of the indicators that educational managers use to measure their effectiveness. Among these are "growth" and "mobility." Are these measures of real or apparent achievement? Can they represent both?

2. Are we inclined to depreciate or criticize the contribution of a previous educational manager as we appreciate the contribution of a new one? Is this always justifiable?

3. Is the typical manager/administrator career expected to be one with ever-increasing responsibility, salary, and title? Is there a basis for more educational managers planning "parabolic" career paths or even shifting career fields at some point?

4. To what extent have major educational managers learned to make effective use of staff specialists? Prepare a staff study of an office indicating how use of staff assistance would make the office more effective.

5. In this chapter we have indicated that a neglected role of the educational manager is that of teaching, of nurturing potential leadership. Describe an educational manager who has the reputation for doing this. How does he do it?

6. To what extent are educational managers employed to fulfill an expectation peculiar to time and place in the history of an organization—to start a new school, to mend broken relationships in an existing institution, to take an institution in a new direction?

NOTES

1. Warren Bennis, "The University Leader," *Saturday Review,* December 1972, p. 43.

2. Eugene E. Jennings, *An Anatomy of Leadership: Princes, Heroes, and Supermen* (New York: McGraw-Hill, 1960), p. 144.

3. Timothy S. Healy, "The Case For Open Admissions: New Problems-New Hopes," *Change,* Summer 1973, p. 29.

4. Clark Kerr, "Administration in An Era of Change and Conflict," *The Educational Record,* Winter 1973, p. 45.

5. Arthur W. Combs, "The Human Aspect of Administration," *Educational Leadership,* November 1970, p. 199.

6. Peter Drucker, *The Effective Executive* (New York: Harper & Row, 1967), p. 25.

Index

The Authors

E. G. Bogue is currently Associate Director for Academic Affairs with the Tennessee Higher Education Commission, the statewide coordinating agency for public higher education. For ten years, Dr. Bogue was on the administrative staff of Memphis State University, the last three years of that appointment as assistant vice president for academic affairs. He also held adjunct faculty appointment in the College of Education at Memphis State and is currently an adjunct faculty member with George Peabody College for Teachers.

Robert L. Saunders is Dean of the College of Education, Memphis State University. Previously he was associate dean of the School of Education, Auburn University. A former public school teacher and principal, Dr. Saunders has been active in a number of special projects and programs aimed at improving the school curriculum and the preparation of teachers. Currently, he serves as the continuing consultant to the Superintendents' Study Council in Tennessee.